Action Replay

Jeffrey Hamm

Action Replay

Jeffrey Hamm

ISBN-13: 978-1-913176-00-6

Sanctuary Press Ltd
71-75 Shelton Street
Covent Garden
London
WC2H 9JQ

www.sanctuarypress.com
Email: info@sanctuarypress.com

Foreword

In the introduction to his autobiography *Left Hand, Right Hand!* Sir Osbert Sitwell says: 'The hour has now struck for me to start on this journey to recapture the past. Already I am nearing fifty and the grey hairs are beginning to show. I have reached the watershed and can see the stream which I must follow downhill toward the limitless ocean ... It is indeed time to begin.'

As yet I have no grey hairs, but I have passed the fifty mark, and so must start on the same journey myself. But why, it may be asked, should I want to write an autobiography at all? To this I answer that, in my opinion, every human life ought to hold enough of interest to merit some record, if only as a contribution to family history. But because the greater part of my life has been spent in the service of the political movements founded and led by Sir Oswald Mosley, both before and after the war of 1939—1945, and because for several years I was closely associated with Sir Oswald as his private secretary, up to his death in December 1980, I believe that the story of my life has a wider interest, and that I write as a witness of events of more than passing significance.

In writing of my wartime experiences in the Falkland Islands and South Africa I have drawn on material contributed by me to *The European*, a magazine of the nineteen-fifties. For the verification of dates and other points of detail I have relied chiefly on *My Life* by Oswald Mosley and *Oswald Mosley* by Robert Skidelsky. My grateful thanks are due to Father Brocard Sewell for helpful advice and for kindly preparing and editing the original typescript, which has subsequently been considerably amended.

Jeffrey Hamm.

1

Chapter One

"Never apologies; say it again and be ruder the second time!" was the advice the elder statesman Lloyd George gave to the young Oswald Mosley, Conservative, Independent and Labour M.P. and junior Minister before founding the British Union of Fascists. Many years later Mosley passed this piece of homespun advice on to me. I trust I have never been unduly rude, but I have certainly never apologised for my membership of British Union and of the post-war Union Movement, nor for being private secretary to Mosley up to his death in December 1980. This book will examine the facts as distinct from the myths and the reader may well agree with me that my life has been a source of modest pride rather than regret.

A holiday in London in 1934 changed my whole life. One Saturday evening I came across a Blackshirt speaker shouting above the din of a howling mob on the corner of Brondesbury Road and Kilburn High Road. I naively asked a particularly noisy interrupter why he did not keep quiet and listen to the speaker. He gave me a reply that set me thinking: "We haven't come to listen to the meeting. We've come to smash it!" At the end of the meeting the Blackshirts marched away to their local headquarters, and I fell in behind them. That was the beginning of a long march which led me to some very strange places: to prison without any charge or trial, and to hospital when I forgot the golden rule of any sport — never to take your eye off the ball. On that occasion the ball was a brick which struck my head and laid me low for several days.

At the end of my holiday I returned to my home in Pontypool in South Wales and subscribed to all the current British Union publications, which I devoured avidly. In one of them I read the striking challenge — 'Those who are not for us are against us' — and I had to decide on which side of the fence I stood. I have never been a mugwump, which has been defined as someone who sits with his mug on one side of the fence and his wump on the other. So in March 1935 I filled in an application form to join the British Union of Fascists, which Sir Oswald Mosley had launched in October 1932 in the hope of creating a modern movement that would achieve — as the old political parties seemed powerless to do — the economic reconstruction that the country so badly needed, through a great programme of economic measures on Keynesian lines, which would solve the unemployment problem through large-scale projects of public works. A number of well-known and respected names in British politics were thinking along these lines and it was not until the later years of pre-war and wartime propaganda that a man or woman holding 'fascist' opinions was generally assumed to be a villain.

What was Fascism? As it was an intensely nationalistic creed it varied considerably from one country to another, and I shall concern myself primarily with the British variety to which I subscribed. Some years ago I was invited to lecture at Sunderland Polytechnic on the origins and development of this 'British' Fascism. It was necessary to discuss Fascist movements in Britain which had preceded the British Union of Fascists. In 1923 a Miss Rotha Lintorn-Orman had founded the British Fascists, joined a year later by the late Arnold Leese, who in 1929 had broken away to form his Imperial Fascist League. So in chronological terms these were the forerunners of British Union, but to what degree did the Mosley movement owe its origins to them? The British Fascists gained some strength during the General Strike of 1926, to which they were strongly opposed, in that age when it was fashionable for Oxbridge undergraduates to drive buses and lorries in strike-breaking activities. But what was Mosley doing during that strike? Leading the Labour Party in Birmingham and addressing innumerable meetings in support of the miners, justifiably striking in protest against cuts in their then miserable wages. This is the first answer to the myth that

Fascism was a right-wing movement. It was in fact a movement of protest against the gross injustices of the capitalist system, and against that communism which attacked it only to substitute its own state capitalism for that of private enterprise.

Arnold Leese certainly had no influence on Mosley, whom he detested. I shall later examine the allegations of anti-Semitism, but Leese had no doubt on the matter: he always referred to Mosley and to those of us who followed him as "kosher Fascists", alleging that we were paid by Jewish interests to propagate a false brand of Fascism, while he personified its pure and undiluted form!

What of the allegation that Mosley's Fascism was copied from Mussolini and Hitler? Mosley's first election address, as a Conservative candidate for Harrow in 1918, contained the extraordinary phrase 'socialistic imperialism', years before anyone had heard of Hitler's 'national socialism.' But if either of these European Fascists had exercised any influence over Mosley, would it have been from the right or from the left? Mussolini had been Editor of a socialist newspaper, and what does the dreaded word 'Nazi' mean? It is, of course, an abbreviation of the long and cumbersome name of the German party, translated into English as 'The National Socialist German Workers' Party'. Nothing very right-wing about that!

But where did British Fascism originate? I profoundly believe the answer I gave the Sunderland students: in the trenches of the first World War. Mosley had served with distinction there and in the air, in the Royal Flying Corps which later became the Royal Air Force. He lost most of his dearest friends in that holocaust and dedicated the rest of his life to attempt to save a future generation from the horrors which he had experienced. He was later joined in British Union by men typical of that flower of British manhood who had not waited for conscription to be introduced, but had volunteered to fight in the war to 'make the world safe for democracy'.

Chapter One

His comrades included the distinguished author Henry Williamson, who wrote so vividly of his war experiences, which left their mark upon him for life. He had taken part in that Christmas Day truce of 1914, when British and German soldiers had cautiously ventured out of their respective trenches, to chat in broken versions of their kindred languages, and to play football, before such dangerous fraternisation was sternly forbidden by the brass-hats in both of the High Commands. On another occasion he had heard a voice crying weakly from a muddy shell-hole and had crawled down to investigate. There he had found a young German soldier, a mere boy, dying of his wounds and in his delirium crying for his mother. Henry had put a comforting arm around the lad, and in halting German had assured him that his mother was there.

These were the soldiers who had been assured by the old men of the Establishment that they would return to 'a land fit for heroes', only to find that they had been cheated and betrayed. The returning ex-serviceman was thrown on to the scrap-heap of unemployment, and officers joined with the men they had commanded in selling matches and bootlaces in the streets of an ungrateful country. In bitterness and cynicism they declared that the promised 'land fit for heroes' had become one in which you had to be a hero to survive. In later years many of them turned to Fascism, in Britain and all over Europe.

I do not propose to set out here a detailed exposition of the pre-war or post-war policies to which I gave my support. These policies have been explained by Mosley in a series of books readily obtainable from public libraries, of which the most notable and fascinating, perhaps, is his autobiography My Life, published in 1968 and currently still in print. This should be supplemented by Professor Robert Skidelsky's biography Oswald Mosley, in the main a very fair and objective study.

However, at a time when it is still fashionable to condone the crimes of Communism and the treacherous antics of its adherents and fellow-travellers within the Establishment, while condemning Fascism and all its works, it is probably necessary that I should explain briefly why I joined Mosley in British Union, and what this cause meant to me personally.

At innumerable public meetings I have spoken in personal terms, relating my political ideas to my early experiences. For instance, as a young student-teacher in Pontypool I had the heartbreaking task of teaching children who had never seen their fathers in work. My friends and neighbours had been abandoned by the old political parties, and left to rot away their lives on street-corners, so that James Maxton, the great socialist and leader of the Independent Labour Party, could justly describe them as "the legions of the lost and the cohorts of the damned."

I used to go every Saturday morning to the weekly session of the magistrates' court in Pontypool, where I listened to the most extraordinary cases. Man after man would shuffle into the dock, to hear the charge read out to him by the clerk of the court: "Stealing a quantity of coal, to the value of one shilling." The 'criminal' was an unemployed miner who had gone to a railway siding where hundreds of rusting trucks were standing, piled high with coal for which there was no market. He had taken a lump of coal, and was running home with it, to light a fire in his empty grate for his wife and children, when he had been arrested. Ridiculous fines would be imposed on these unhappy men, which of course they could not pay. In default, they trooped off to Cardiff Prison, week after week.

In the same period of this shameful betrayal of Britain by the Conservative Party — thinly disguised in 1931 as the 'National' Government — I used to attend Labour Party meetings, and listen to our M.P., Arthur Jenkins, denounce the evils of life in Germany under Hitler, or later in Spain under Franco, while only the previous Sunday he had read in chapel the lesson which advised us to cast out the mote in our own eye before examining the beam in others. (While I was at school in Pontypool

Chapter One

Arthur Jenkins's son Roy, was at his school in neighbouring Aberscychan. He did not then speak with the accent and lisp he acquired and carefully cultivated in later years).

Before I examine those childhood years, let me emphasise that it was in revolt against this state of things that I became 'an angry young man', some twenty years before the phrase was thought of, and turned to Fascism, which was to me, as to so many others, basically an economic creed. Policies made sense to me which advocated forbidding the export of capital from the City of London, which in the thirties was investing its money in countries where wages were lowest and hours of work longest, so as to draw a high rate of interest.

Successive British governments allowed the good produced in the Far East by sweated labour to flood back into Britain, undercutting British industry and causing widespread unemployment. I saw the tragic absurdity of that system in South Wales, and also in Lancashire, where the unemployed textile worker went off with the dole in his pocket to the corner shop, there to buy a Japanese shirt. Fascism was to me simply a revolt against that system, advancing the alternative policy of compelling the City to invest in British industry and to re-equip it with modern machinery, while forbidding the importation of any goods which could be produced in Britain. The policy of British Union was summarised in such slogans as 'Britain First!' and 'Britain for the British!' Should I now apologise for having embraced such a patriotic, nationalist creed? I shall never offer any apology, for none is due. "Never apologise; say it again and be ruder the second time!".

Chapter Two

"Neither fish, flesh, nor fowl", said the Bishop of the Falkland Islands, when he heard that I had been born in Monmouthshire, which has now been given back its former Welsh name of Gwent. I had met him after taking up an appointment as a travelling teacher in the Falklands, before my wartime arrest and detention there under Defence Regulation 18B.

Those of us born and bred in the old Monmouthshire were never in any doubt that we were Welsh, but perhaps we shared the confusion of the English legislators who spoke of 'South Wales and Monmouthshire' and included the old Assizes at Monmouth, and later in Newport, in the English Oxford Circuit. The same legislators paid lip-service to the Welsh nonconformist conscience by closing the pubs of Gwent on Sundays, while allowing the clubs to remain open. We were truly Cymric, even though few of us could speak more than a few words of the hen Iaith, the old language — one of the oldest in Europe.

In the Falkland Islands I met a German wartime internee who had been obliged for years to travel on a Czech passport, but had always insisted: "My papers may say I'm a Czech, but my heart says I'm a German!" My own heart paid no attention to disputed boundaries between England and Wales, but assured me with every beat that I was Welsh.

Yet I had an English father, and bear the English name of Hamm, a common name in Somerset, where my father's family had farmed for generations. As a young man he had crossed the Bristol Channel to work in South Wales, where he had married a girl with the not uncommon name of Jones. This mixed origin has perhaps been beneficial, protecting me from infection with extreme nationalism, or racialism, so that my patriotism has never taken the form of despising those who have suffered the misfortune of being born outside Wales. For most of my life I have been associated with politics and policies which have been branded 'extremist' and even 'racialist', but I know such labels to be ill-deserved. If I have any racial prejudices, they tend to take the form of a perhaps disproportionate affection for certain other countries, peoples and languages.

I was born in Ebbw Vale, in the Western Valley of Gwent, and moved as a small child first to Monmouth, close to the English border, and then to Pontypool, in the Eastern Valley, where I spent most of my youth. Consequently, my memories of Ebbw Vale are blurred, although I have returned there many times over the years. I have a natural affection for this town that gave me birth, a town of coal and steel. Memories of Monmouth are more vivid, while every street in Pontypool, and every road and lane in the countryside around it, is as real to me as if I had lived there all my life.

The house in Ebbw Vale in which I was born is well known to all familiar with the town, not because a commemorative plaque marks the historic spot, but because of its position. It stands next to the Roman Catholic church on Tredegar Road, one of three red-brick houses my grandfather built. In my childhood days, in that age of horse-drawn transport, the house stood next to a Co-operative Society stables which later became a garage when horses gave place to motor-vans. The church was built long after we had left the town.

Do we really remember our childhood? Or do we in later years relate, embellished in the telling, only the tales our parents told us? From my own memories, and later promptings, I can recall a confused picture of my early days at school. Some years ago I went back to look for the old building, but it had long been demolished. From these confused memories there emerges a self-portrait, no doubt much distorted, of a small boy playing cricket in the back-yard, or sitting in chapel on a Sunday evening, fidgeting through a too-long sermon until I announced in a too-loud voice that I wanted to go home. "Soon", my mother would whisper. "No, not soon, NOW!", would be my reply, in a still louder and fiercer voice. I was an impatient child, the embryo of an impatient man.

My father, Clifford Hamm, was a clerk in the offices of the Ebbw Vale Steel, Iron and Coal Company, both before and after the first World War, in which he served in the 10th Battalion of the South Wales Borderers. But he remained very much the Englishman, and clung doggedly to his English pronunciations, which sounded quaint to ears attuned to the Welsh lilt and South Wales expressions. No doubt he was a kindly man at heart, but I found him taciturn, and at no time was there much real communication between us.

I have a mental picture of him, on a Sunday morning, sitting huddled over the fire in our ancient range, engrossed in the sports pages of the News of the World. In later years I thought, with the arrogance of youth, that this ill-equipped him to dispute with me the politics which I had embraced, and which he violently rejected. All this has brought much comfort to those psychiatrists, amateur or professional, to whom I have related these childhood impressions. They have all been convinced that here lies the simple explanation for my adopting 'authoritarian' politics. They see life in such simple terms, but I have found it complicated, and often contradictory. I have been card-indexed by them, and filed away with all the other poor lost souls who have suffered a 'deprived' childhood and have then gone on to adolescence and manhood searching for a 'leader', a father-figure to replace the father whom they had rejected, or who had rejected them.

My mother, Gladys, was a kindly and simple soul, and to her, I was devoted. I make this admission at the risk of being again laid on the psychiatrist's couch, to rise with yet another label tied neatly round my neck, that of 'a mother's boy'. Perhaps we do indeed lack the grace to see ourselves as others see us, but what I know of myself seems to me to bear little resemblance to either of the above descriptions.

I had no brothers, but one sister, Vera, born in Pontypridd in 1910. From there my parents moved to Ebbw Vale, where I was born on 15 September 1915, a war-baby, my father being abroad on active service at the time. I have frequently been told that when he eventually came home on leave I registered my disapproval of this intruder in the strongest possible terms, and that this was the cause of the disharmony between us.

My mother's father, Edward Jones, was a builder and undertaker, assisted by his two sons and my grandmother, who kept the accounts. From my grandfathers, maternal and paternal, I received my names of Edward Jeffrey, although it is by the latter that I have always been called.

I have only vague memories of my father's family, although I spent several happy boyhood holidays with them in Somerset, and in later life stayed in London with one of my father's five brothers and his family. This Somerset influence was to play a part in my life. My father had never lost his love for his origins in the countryside, and in 1923 he uprooted us from Ebbw Vale to move to Monmouth, where he rented a poultry farm. No ties now remain to bind me to Ebbw Vale, and it is some years since I last paid a nostalgic visit to the town. I called at the house where I was born and then walked to Beaufort, between Ebbw Vale and Brynmawr, to the cemetery where my grandparents rest. To find a particular Jones grave in a Welsh cemetery seemed a hopeless task, but the attendant had known the family and led me to the spot, sadly neglected and overgrown with weeds. We cleared them away, and I stood for a few minutes, reading the inscription on the headstones. From the cemetery I climbed the hillside to that miniature Stonehenge erected in memory of Tredegar's famous son and Ebbw Vale's M.P. for many years, Aneurin Bevan: gaunt boulders irreverently known as 'Nye's

Gallstones', reaching up towards the storm-clouds never long absent from any Welsh mountain. Then down into Tredegar, and back again to the highest point, with its clear view of Tredegar on one side and Ebbw Vale on the other. Was it on this spot that Nye conjured up the graphic phrase that government should control 'the commanding heights of the economy'?

Chapter Three

"My old man said 'Follow the Van'," goes a once-popular ditty. Did we really travel from Ebbw Vale to Monmouth in May 1923 in the front seat of the van carrying our furniture, as I seem to remember? Or was it in a car which followed the van ?

By some form of transport we arrived in Monmouth, and at our new home, Yew Tree Bungalow, on the Kymin, that hill overlooking the town, on the other side of the river, with its views of Gloucestershire and Herefordshire, to preserve the old county names of relevance and significance. By car one leaves Monmouth by Wye Bridge, and continues along the Coleford Road, towards the Forest of Dean, before turning right to begin the steep ascent. The road does not wind, but jerks its way uphill in a series of long, straight stretches and sharp right-angled bends. Up the first straight and turn sharp left. Up the second straight, passing the poplar trees on your left, and then turn sharp right. Up the third straight, passing the old yew tree which stood opposite the gate of our bungalow and gave it its name. Two more right-angle bends and you reach the flat grassy top and an eccentric folly-tower, a monument to England's admirals, erected there because of Nelson's long association with the town of Monmouth, where he used to be a guest of the Hamiltons.

Names of famous admirals and their battle-honours were carved on plaques around a 'temple' which stood on the summit of the Kymin. We were proud of our little town, with its Agincourt Square, commemorating the victory of Monmouth's famous son Henry V, 'Harry of Monmouth', born in the castle whose ruins overlook the square. Let no detractors suggest that it was really "A-gjn-court' Square, so called because hotels and public houses bordered it on three sides. We would hear of no such heresies as we stood and stared up at Henry's statue, a sceptre in his hand, high up on the wall of the old Assize building, from where he looks down on another statue, standing on the ground, that of Henry Rolls, of Rolls-Royce fame.

School holidays are always a boy's delight, and this seemed to be especially so in Monmouth. Thousands of trees to climb, and birds' nests to be raided and eggs to be 'blown' before being placed with loving care in glass show-cases. Mushrooms to be picked in the early morning, with the dew fresh and wet on the grass, through which new shoots appeared as we worked. Blackberrying throughout the long, hot summer days, and large baskets of luscious blackberries to be carried into town, for sale to the travelling representative of a jam manufacturer, who paid us the fabulous sum of one penny (in pre-metric currency) per pint or pound, so that we could earn a whole bright shining shilling, or even greater wealth, for a day's back-breaking and finger-scratching work.

There was no transport to school, so my sister and I walked the mile and a half each way. Going to school of a morning was comparatively easy, as it was downhill most of the way, and we were refreshed after a night's sleep, but the return journey was always an ordeal. In winter we trudged through snowdrifts which almost engulfed us, while in summer we dragged our tired little feet up the hill. My sister and I shared a satchel or case, and there was some elaborate arrangement between us whereby we carried it in turn, on alternative days or alternate stretches of the long and dusty road, but I was only seven and she was twelve, so it always seemed to be my turn to do the portering. Occasionally I would rebel, dumping the satchel by the roadside, leaving it far behind me, vowing that nothing would induce me to go back for it. But her will-power was stronger than mine, and I was always forced to give way, returning unwillingly to retrieve the burden, and bringing it back with even slower footsteps.

The long walk home made us hungry, and at appropriate seasons of the year we would slip into a field beside the road, lift a turnip, carrot or swede, and break off the top, which we would replace in the ground, thus leaving no evidence of our foray, before continuing to munch our way homewards. In summer there would be wild strawberries to pick from the roadside banks, whose grass and ferns concealed many a cunningly hidden wren's or robin's nest. When eventually we staggered indoors our day was far from done.

There was no running water on the Kymin; rainwater for washing was collected in tanks and barrels, but our drinking-water had to be fetched from a pump in the woods, half-way between our bungalow and the main road. With large jug or bucket in hand, and much resentment in our hearts, we would set out for the pump, which often ran dry in summer. In winter it froze, and we would heat a poker white-hot, run with it, before it cooled, to the pump and plunge it into the ice to thaw it out and get the ancient mechanism working again. Life was hard in a bungalow with no running water. We had to bath in a tub filled with rainwater and heated over an old-fashioned range. The only lavatory was in the garden, well away from the bungalow for hygienic reasons, since it had, of course, no running water: only a bucket which had to be emptied periodically. Modern country-dwellers and town and city folk know nothing of the joys of rural life in the nineteen twenties and thirties.

My years in Monmouth laid the foundation of what little formal education I ever received, for I never went on from school to university or college. I have never underrated the advantages to be derived from a university education, but I have consoled myself for its absence by believing that great truths are often concealed in clichés. Certainly I have learned much from the 'University of Life', and also from what many of its graduates claim to be the finest university in the world: prison.

At the age of seven, with little previous education, I went to Monmouth Intermediate School, a sort of unofficial preparatory establishment for Monmouth School, where I was introduced to

Chapter Three

French, an innovation decades ahead of the prevailing custom of no foreign languages before the ages of eleven or twelve. During school holidays I often accompanied my father to the Friday market, where our eggs and other produce were taken in a cart drawn by a wild-eyed mare of unpredictable habits. Perhaps of unpredictable sex too, for she was always called Tom.

She would take fright at a passing car or a piece of paper blown across the road, and back would go her ears as she bolted, with the unfortunate driver tugging at the reins. On one occasion a farm-boy bailed out, jumping overboard into the hedge, abandoning ship and cargo. Tom was eventually stopped in the town, and returned to us by her captor. We often arrived late at the market, because Tom had been in a particularly frisky mood and had defied efforts to corner her for harnessing. My father would be in the market for hours, or so it seemed to me at the time, and I would be left outside holding the bridle of the fiery steed, which tossed its head impatiently, snorting and flashing its eyes at me. I was terrified of the animal, but I never deserted my post.

For some obscure reason we kept another horse, a heavy dray, on the plot of land around our bungalow. What, a horse in the garden? Yes, and this is no trick of memory. How could I ever forget the night when it slipped into a ditch between the field and the bungalow, with a crash which shook the building and almost tumbled us out of our beds? It took much heaving, pulling and pushing to get 'Old Duke', as he was called, back on to terra firma.

I learned to ride both horses bare-back, and also an assortment of other animals, including a pig. With this animal I did not have a great deal of success since its curved back was no help to little legs, struggling to grip its slippery and hairy sides. In later years I took up riding again, and got a great deal of pleasure from it. My ability to ride played some part in taking me to South America and unexpected adventures.

Alas, our rural life was to last for two or three years only. In the nineteen-twenties farming was in the doldrums, and prices for eggs were abysmally low. My poor father became poorer, his small savings being swallowed up by bills for foodstuffs and so on. Fate appeared to be against him. In those primitive days young chicks were kept alive by means of a lamp in their box. The lamp would often go out during the night, and the chicks would huddle together for warmth, in a frenzied struggle for survival in which the weakest would be trampled underfoot and only the strongest survived. Poultry diseases decimated our stock, and my father was reluctantly forced to sell the lease of the farm and to consider returning to life and work in the town. Before we left Monmouth we had moved to a pleasant house, Wye View, near the foot of the Kymin, and overlooking the Coleford road and the farm, which ran down to the old Dixon Road.

The years at Monmouth left their mark on me, inspiring a love of the town's historical associations and of the beauty of the Wye valley and the surrounding countryside. From my little school we had gone on trips up the Wye as far as Symonds Yat, with its towering Seven Sisters rocks, and downstream to the haunting ruins of Tintern Abbey. I have seen the rocks and the abbey again in later years, and have walked from Chepstow up the Wye to a height commanding a wonderful view of both Wye and Severn. On occasions, some appropriate and others less so, memories of Monmouth's history have come flooding back. One summer's afternoon, a few years ago, at the Regent's Park Open Air Theatre, I was enraptured as Esmond Knight held his audience spellbound with his monologue The Archer's Tale, the story of Agincourt told in the words of one of those who had sailed to France with Harry of Monmouth, and had there pulled the long bow. And in my later political life, at the height of a street battle during a rowdy public meeting, I have sometimes rallied my supporters, often sorely outnumbered by a highly organised and violent communist opposition, with Harry's cry before Agincourt: "But we few in it shall be remembered. We few, we happy few, we band of brothers."

Chapter Four

Ponerpoo Free Prayer! Ponerpoo Free Prayer!" What a strange incantation was this, calling the faithful to pray without charge in some Welsh mosque? We had moved from Monmouth to Pontypool in December 1925, three months after my tenth birthday and shortly before Christmas. The school term was at or near its end, and I was on holiday until the New Year. It was a Friday morning, and as I lay in bed the strange chanting began again: "Ponerpoo free prayer! Ponerpoo free prayer!" It was, I discovered, a paper-boy on his rounds, selling the local Pontypool Free Press, calling potential customers to their doors in what the Welsh rugby star Gerald Davies calls, in his autobiography, 'the Pontypool drawl', for in language also we were 'neither fish, flesh, nor fowl', speaking, so our critics declared, neither Welsh nor English. Years later, at the London Welsh Association in Grays Inn Road, at our Welsh classes, a Pontypool girl and myself were teased with the gibe that when we first came to London we had both had to have elocution lessons, as no one could understand us, because of our lazy habit of slurring our words and dropping their final syllables.

We now lived at No.16 Brynwern, in a council house. Brynwern stands at the top of the town, at the foot of the Tranch, on the western side of the Eastern Valley, as it runs from Newport to Blaenavon. There was a view across the narrow town to Penygarn, on the opposite hillside. Years later, on a day when Pontypool were playing rugby against London Welsh at the Old Deer Park, an old friend of my youth was trying to refresh the memory of another old Pontypool boy who could not recall me. "You must remember Jeffrey", he said. "He was a boy from the top." Indeed I was; and so were all my neighbours, all boys from the top, to which we climbed from town and school, up the steep hill to our homes, to which we were alleged to cling with the bushy eyebrows some of us developed. Brynwern was a pleasant place, not at all like the modern council estate. There were no monstrous tower-blocks, but neat semi-detached houses that ran not in straight lines but in gentle curves easy upon the eye. The first few houses formed a square, and then continued in a reasonably straight line until they turned a corner, on which stood No. 16, looking towards the hill which ran down to Crane Street and the town centre. At about No. 21 the street turned another corner and ran round in a wide semi-circle, until it emerged and straightened again. 'The Circle', a field of little grass but many stones, was our playing field, on which we sought to emulate the exploits of our heroes of the Pontypool rugby team, which then played on the Recreation Ground, off the Circle. In summer we played cricket on the same patch, when we became our other heroes, the Pontypool Cricket Eleven, who played in the Park. (The rugby club now plays there, too). The local derby was between Brynwem and neighbouring Edward Street, a match which usually ended in fighting, with the Brynwern boys chasing their rivals back to their lair in Edward Street, with sticks and stones. Mother disapproved of such ungentlemanly behaviour.

In January 1926 I started school in Pontypool, and came down to earth from the dizzy heights of Monmouth's Intermediate School. Instead, I had to attend an old-fashioned elementary school — as they were then called — at Park Terrace, and I remained there throughout that year. But building was in progress on a modern school, to be called Twmpath Central School. This forerunner of the later comprehensives was just a few minutes' walk from my home, at the foot of the Tranch, and I enrolled there when it opened in January 1927.

Within a few months I had sat and passed the entrance examination for 'West Mon', as it was always called. The more famous Monmouth School had been founded by one William Jones of the Worshipful Company of Haberdashers, and the money left over after its foundation had been placed in trust for the building of further schools, including two in Monmouth.

That town is tucked away in a north-east corner of the county, and the Company cherished the idea of building another school in West Monmouthshire, to cater for boys from that side of the county. At some stage 'Squire' Hanbury, a magnate of the Welsh tin-plate industry, made a generous offer of free or cheap land in Pontypool, and it was there that the school was built. But it was given the name its founders had already chosen, and became West Monmouth School, despite being located in the dead centre of the county.

In my days, its Head attended the Public Schools Headmasters' Conference, which entitled it to be listed as a public school, even if it was overshadowed by others much better known. Its intake was only ninety boys a year, and there was keen annual competition for these places from the whole of the Eastern Valley of Monmouthshire. I passed my entrance examination in the summer of 1927, and was placed 18th, which entitled me to a free place in the school, and free books.

From my first day there in September 1927 a magic carpet was displayed before our eyes, and we were reminded of it constantly, indeed almost daily, for the next four years. It was labelled 'London Matric', and to step upon its golden fleece one had to pass the then Oxford School Certificate examination, with credits — these were higher than the pass marks — in at least five subjects, of which English and Mathematics were compulsory. Matriculation was more than a magic carpet; it was, we were constantly assured, a golden key which would open every gate to Paradise, via the Sixth Form, the Higher School Certificate, and then college or university.

The examination fetish is now out of fashion, although the report Aspects of Secondary Education in England: A Survey by H.M. Inspectors of Schools, issued on 5 December 1979, establishes that it has retained its grip on many schools. In my schooldays it was a carrot which encouraged many an old donkey to plod through classwork and homework in the days of 'swotting', and of learning facts and figures by heart or rule of thumb. We may not have emerged from this system much the wiser, but certainly 'much better informed', as F. E. Smith said to the judge. (Mr. FE. Smith - later Lord Birkenhead - once had to explain the same point several times to a rather dim-witted judge, who still sighed and said: " I am no wiser, Mr. Smith!" To which the learned counsel replied: "No, my Lord, but much better informed!")

How frightened but how proud we were on our first day, as we walked up Blaendare Road and through the sacred gates, along the terrace beside the velvet lawn, and into the great hall. Our grey flannel trousers carried creases which would not have disgraced the Welsh Guards, our shoes were polished until they would have gladdened the heart of a sergeant-major in that proud regiment, while our blazers, bearing the arms and motto of the Haberdashers' Company were immaculate. That motto, 'Serve and Obey', has proved appropriate to my chosen life-style in politics.

We were subjected to some rough and ready initiation ceremonies by the older boys, but we all survived, and did not suffer the ill-effects which are supposed to haunt the bullied throughout life. Soon we were swaggering about the school, and through the town with the airs and graces of those who imagine themselves superior to lesser mortals: in this instance, boys from other schools less favoured. The work was hard, and I struggled through my first three years with no academic distinction, relieved to be allowed at the end of them to enter the Form V Arts of my choice. But life at West Mon was not all work. We had lessons all day on Mondays, Wednesdays and Fridays, and Tuesday, Thursday and Saturday mornings, with games on those three afternoons. I took little part in the cricket season, but rugby brought me to life, out of my summer sloth. There might be three matches a week, for Form and House on Tuesdays and Thursdays, and for the School 2nd XV on Saturdays, as one rose to the dizzy heights of possible inclusion in the School First XV.

Not a waking moment outside school was to be wasted. In term-time, homework took up much of the evenings, and I was further occupied by serving as errand boy for a gents' outfitters in the town, the firm of Douglas Welch of Abergavenny. I continued with this part-time job until the pressures of homework became too acute; it involved getting up early to clean the shop window or scrub the doorstep on my way to school: and hurrying back to the shop after school in order to deliver hats to the local gentry.

My undistinguished academic career must have taxed the wits of form-masters who had to think of some suitable comment to write on my reports. Later on I found myself facing the same unenviable task in the various boarding schools where I was employed as a teacher. However, I never tried to emulate one of my colleagues who wrote on the end-of-year report of a boy who had been consistently bottom of the form: "He has maintained his position throughout the year." Another classic witticism of this kind was made by the Reverend Montague Summers, historian of Restoration drama and the Gothic novel. When Summers was teaching at Brockley County School about 1922 the Headmaster expressed surprise at a staff meeting that Mr. Summers had awarded sixty marks to a boy of abysmal academic attainments. Summers explained that he had indeed given the boy sixty marks out of a hundred: twenty for carelessness, twenty for idleness, and twenty for ignorance.

My own form-masters lacked such wit, or malice, and contented themselves with a standard formula which never varied: "He is a prolific reader of the form library." Indeed I was. I read widely, if not always well, and devoured everything from the classics to the latest thriller by Edgar Wallace, bought for a penny or so, in a tattered second-hand, paperback edition, from a bookshop in the town. I would also sit for hours in the public library, reading the magazines of the period: the Strand, Wide World, the National Geographical Magazine, and others.

A favourite holiday or weekend pastime was walking, and within a few years of arriving in Pontypool I had walked everywhere within a radius of ten or fifteen miles. I had no fear of walking through the darkness of the night across a Welsh mountain-top. We never seemed to hear of assaults on children. Did they never occur, or were we oblivious to them? My parents never warned me against such dangers, as far as I can remember. If they did, my stubbornness must have worn them down, for they allowed me to continue my wanderings.

So life continued in this agreeable fashion until the dreaded School Certificate Examination loomed ominously near. If I doubted my ability to pass, I was not helped by my father's insistence, delivered with many an expressive shaking of his head, that I was an idiot, and stood no chance at all. I bitterly resented his attitude; but in retrospect I wonder if he were not perhaps applying some elementary psychological pressure on me, in the belief that his abuse would goad me to greater effort.

His final ruse, which probably had the same end in view, was to bet me some, for those days, fabulous sum — it might be ten shillings — that I would not pass. That did the trick! For the three months before the examination I scarcely went out of the house, except to school, so that certain friends who did not attend my school thought that I had died. I lived the life of a hermit, shut away in my bedroom night after night, poring over the books which had been disgracefully neglected in favour of sport.

Our masters believed in the methods of the period, now so largely discredited; not least the benefits to be derived from much learning by heart. (Why this highly cerebral activity should be associated with the symbolic seat of the affections is obscure). The history master, in particular, produced sensational results year after year by twin methods. The first was to study previous School Cert, examination papers, note the sequence of questions, and spot with uncanny accuracy, those likely to be repeated in the next year's papers. As a further aid to preparation for the examination he used to hand us duplicated lists of the main points required to answer the previously-listed questions.

We could all recite them by heart and remember them sufficiently well to write identical answers. Perhaps it was not education, but it produced results.

The examinations came and went, and I tried to put them out of my mind as I enjoyed the long, hot summer of 1931. I was sitting on a grassy bank in Pontypool Park, watching cricket, when my parents brought to me the news that the results had arrived by post. I had passed, and had gained the much-coveted credits in my five subjects, giving me exemption from the London University Matriculation Examination, and the right to enter the Sixth Form in September. I entered it with the intention of studying English, French, German and Latin for my Higher School Certificate, hoping to go on to read modern languages at university. But this was not to be, for my father continued to criticise and oppose the idea of my further education.

In retrospect again, I should recall charitably that he was now earning a very small wage as an insurance agent, and therefore felt entitled to ask why I was not leaving school and going out into the world to earn some money, to supplement the meagre family income. Yet miners' sons and daughters, and even the children of the unemployed, were going up to Oxford or Cambridge, helped by scholarships, grants being as yet unknown, so perhaps I should have been given my chance. I have no deep regret at not having gone up to university, but I sometimes wonder what effect it might have had upon me, and whether I would have made any impression there. Instead, after some six months in the Sixth Form I left abruptly, grasping at any straw, and finding employment for which I was utterly unsuited.

Those last six months at school were the happiest of my stay there, for I suddenly discovered a milieu in which I could hold my own against all comers. I had won no prizes for sport or for academic subjects, but now a new world of opportunity opened before me, one which has influenced the whole of my political life. Perhaps I was a late developer; possibly if I had left school

Chapter Four

before entering the Sixth Form no one outside my small circle of friends would have known of my existence there. But in the Sixth I joined two school organisations which influenced me greatly: the school Debating Society and the school branch of the League of Nations Union, which supported the League just as the United Nations Association now supports the League's successor, the United Nations Organisation.

There was a school magazine, The Westmonion, which appeared annually. Perhaps because of my undistinguished record in the lower forms I have preserved one issue only, that for the academic year 1931-32. It is now tattered with much handling, possibly through my nonchalantly showing it to unsuspecting friends, hoping that they would find the appropriate pages, on which my praises were sung in rather extravagant schoolboy prose.

The magazine reported my first speech in debate, the first in my life, the forerunner of many more in later years, on street corners, in university debates, in Trafalgar Square. I had been asked to oppose the motion: "This house believes that modern civilisation is heading for destruction", and with that supreme optimism which has never deserted me I agreed to do so. I had written out my speech in full and learned it by heart, so that I needed only to give it an occasional glance while I was delivering it. The motion was defeated, so my maiden speech helped to carry the day. My record read, in sporting terms: played one, won one.

The next meeting of the Debating Society took the form of a mock election, and I was asked to be the supporting speaker for one of the candidates. After recording that this candidate's speech had been given a noisy reception, the magazine continued: "E.J. Hamm followed with the best speech of the evening; with all the facts on his finger-tips, he gained the confidence of the whole House, and sat down amid loud applause."

Our candidate was duly elected, with an overwhelming majority, a success I have never been able to repeat in the political field.

The Debating Society's final meeting in that year was devoted to a light-hearted mock trial, an action for breach of promise of marriage, common in the courts in those days, before they were abolished. Counsel for the plaintiff was the senior history master, who later became headmaster, while I appeared for the defendant, in whose favour the jury duly found. As the history master had also been called to the Bar, although he did not practice, I regarded my victory with perhaps justifiable pride. My final score in debate thus stood at: played three, won three. The Westmonion, in its Sixth Form Activities feature, was kind enough to comment: "In the Debating Society, Hamm was outstanding."

Our fathers had served in the first World War, and we had listened with horror to their harrowing tales of trench warfare and mass casualties in pointless battles, where 'someone had blundered.' In our youthful idealism we yearned for a world where there would be no more war. This idealism was nourished by books, films and plays, such as Journey's End, All Quiet on the Western Front, and Kameradschaft. I was tremendously influenced by the poetry of Hubert Brooke and Siegfried Sassoon. So we enthusiastically set up a school branch of the League of Nations Union, and I became its Treasurer. The boy who founded the branch won a national essay prize which entitled him to a holiday in Geneva, where he attended meetings of the League, its committees and secretariats. He returned to school with an added zeal for peace, and helped to organise a 'mock assembly' of the League, at which I recall boys making speeches in French, German and Esperanto, for which we had one enthusiast.

My League of Nations Union activities gained for me the only prize that I received in the course of my undistinguished school career. One meeting was devoted to impromptu speeches. The entrants had to wait in an ante-room, where they could not hear the previous speakers. Then they entered, one by one, and were given a piece of paper bearing the chosen subject on which they were to speak, for five minutes. My paper read: "Can the

League of Nations end War?" I enthusiastically argued that it could. Alas, in 1939 it was proved that on this occasion at least my optimism had been misplaced. But my effort won me the prize, and I was presented with a copy of Sir Norman Angell's The Great Illusion. For years I clung to my faith in the ideals of the League of Nations, but even in my earliest speeches at school I was questioning some of its decisions. The League appeared to me even then to be an instrument for maintaining the European post-war status quo, perpetuating the injustices of the Treaty of Versailles, which seemed all too likely to bring about a new war, unless they were remedied. But in voicing such opinions within the school I seemed to be an odd-man-out, destined perhaps to follow in later years an independent line as an advocate of unpopular policies — unpopular at least in orthodox and Establishment circles.

For me, my last year at school really did constitute 'the happiest days of my life', an unusual experience, it would seem. Since then, like everyone, I have experienced grief and sadness, but this has been balanced by much deep and lasting happiness. The day came when I handed in my textbooks, emptied my desk, and walked through the school gates for the last time as a pupil. I walked down Blaendare Road, through the town, and so home, with thoughts of seeking in the outside world a fame and fortune which have always eluded me.

What influence did my formative years at West Mon have on me? In general that influence has been good. It gave me, for instance, that self-confidence which a public school, however minor, bestows on all who pass through its system. Less happy was the absurd snobbery which the headmaster of my day tried to instil in his charges. He was an Oxford man, and intensely proud of the fact. When I visited him some years after leaving I found him still seething with indignation over an application he had received for a teaching post which had been advertised some months previously. What had occurred to displease him so? "A Cambridge man" had applied, he explained, with indignant hauteur, "A Cambridge man. I wouldn't have one in my kitchen!" Oh, unfortunate creature, to have imagined that he could enter West Mon from 'that other place.'

I trust that the good influences of the school have lingered on, and continue to influence me, while I hope that I have been able to get rid of the snobbery and other unsatisfactory attitudes acquired in what was basically a very fine school. I got to appreciate at quite an early age the absurdity of so-called 'class', whether of the Left or of the Right in conventional politics and society. I came to despise the snobbery of the Right, and the equally absurd inverted snobbery of the Left, symbolised by the boiled shirt of Conservatism and the red shirt of International Socialism and Communism. I came to prefer the black shirt of a classless movement, and threw myself into the realities of a struggle for social justice, rather than into the mock battles of class warfare.

Chapter Five

"Had I but followed the arts", sighed Sir Andrew Aguecheek in Twelfth Night. I had followed them throughout my school career, when I had dreaded science lessons and had found them an intolerable bore. So to what job did I turn in desperation, in the hope of earning a little money. I answered a newspaper advertisement for an assistant in a chemist's shop in Newport, and it was there that I started work.

The shop stood at the top of Stow Hill, and there I climbed each day after my early morning bus journey from Pontypool, returning home late in the evening, especially on Saturdays: six days a week except for the Thursday half-day. The pharmacist, a Mr. Frost, tried hard to initiate me into the mysteries of dispensing, and I learned the rudiments from a book of simple prescriptions. I soon lost any faith I might have had in medicines when I learned that one usually filled the bottle to its neck with water, before adding a few drops of some liquid which could do little good but no harm, and was brightly coloured and pleasant to the taste. With no qualifications, I was allowed to dispense only under the supervision of the pharmacist. I found wrapping the bottles more difficult than making up the contents. In the evenings I used to be sent home with a bottle and a pile of wrapping-paper, to practice wrapping it round the bottle neatly, and rounding it off, with razor-sharp edges, to the part which tapered to a point above the cork. I spent much time and used up much paper, but I never mastered the art; my fingers did not seem to be designed for practical work. For this and other reasons the pharmacist and I decided, after only seven weeks, that I had embarked upon the wrong profession; so we parted company, by mutual agreement.

Then followed months of unemployment, spent in heartbreaking search for work in the South Wales of the depression years, now back again after a further fifty years of old-party misgovernment. I applied for any job I saw advertised, however menial. An advertisement in an evening paper invited applications for the post of booking-clerk at a Newport coach depot. Applicants were required to present themselves for an interview at 9 o'clock the following morning. I was up early, and on the bus for Newport. A dash from the bus station to the office, and there I saw a queue of hopefuls, winding around the block. I joined the queue, which moved in slow crocodile towards the office where the interviews were being conducted. The pace grew faster, and applicants were in and out within minutes. When my turn came, I found out why: we were being told that seventy or more candidates had already been interviewed, but that we could leave our names and addresses if we wished. I left my own particulars, returned home, and heard no more. Fate had decided that it was not my destiny to be a booking-clerk in a Newport bus depot.

So I turned to teaching, then the poor man's profession in South Wales, as elsewhere. Even today, what school in England does not have at least one Welsh master on its staff? I was allowed to enter the noble profession as a student teacher, unpaid, at Town School, long demolished, but then standing near Crane Street station, itself demolished when the Beeching axe cut off all railway lines up the Welsh valleys.

There was a glorious theory that you served as a student teacher to gain practical experience during the few months while you were waiting for admission to a teachers' training college. But there is often a wide gap between theory and practice, and so there was in my case. Competition for entry to college was intense, because the number of applicants far exceeded the vacancies; so you applied for a paid post as an 'uncertificated assistant' until the happy day dawned and you entered college, to emerge 'certificated.'

On Saturday mornings the Director of Education for Monmouthshire held court in his office in Newport's County

Hall, and I would travel there every three or four weeks, to sit for hours in a waiting-room, moving up one place at a time, as if in a crowded doctor's surgery. One was in and out quite as quickly as one is in the latter establishments when a harassed medical locum tenens is confronted with an unexpected influenza epidemic. The Director would open the door of his room to you with one hand, while he put his other arm around your shoulder in a fatherly gesture. The door would close behind you, and he would shepherd you across his office, murmuring soothing words about having no vacancy "at present", and the possibility that something might turn up soon. At the same time he was propelling you towards an exit door, which he would open with his free hand. It was all done with such old-world charm and courtesy, so typical of the Welsh, that you could not take offence. Not even when you heard, a few days later, that the son or nephew of a Labour councillor had found a paid post, or been admitted to college, thus jumping the queue or leapfrogging over you.

I had a real and passionate love of teaching which made me endure all these slings and arrows of a particularly outrageous fortune, so that I persevered, unpaid, for nearly three years. Whenever possible I volunteered to teach the most troublesome class in the school, in days when there were few if any Special Schools, and the sadly subnormal sat with normal pupils in an overcrowded classroom. I often wonder what happened to the poor disturbed lad who used to crawl round the room and bite the ankles of the unwary. Perhaps he is now in Parliament, shouting abuse across the gangway.

I loved these wilder spirits, and I trust I had some influence on them. I joined enthusiastically in their games, and allowed them, to their great delight, to tackle me furiously in our games of rugby. Perhaps it was for this reason that the Head gave me a reference which included the following encomium: "His discipline is firm yet kind. A keen sportsman, he is tremendously popular with the children, while his willingness to work and pleasant demeanour have endeared him to the staff." Praise indeed, although somewhat flattering.

But what had happened to my desire to contribute to the family budget? I was able to get a lot of work coaching backward children, or cramming brighter ones for their scholarship examinations, and in this way I earned enough to keep myself and save for an annual holiday in London. However, a neighbour in Brynwern — a former schoolfellow at West Mon, but four or five years older than myself, and in a higher form — was bringing pressure to bear on me to change my occupation.

Jack was a clever, indeed a brilliant boy, held up to us at school, in many a glowing tribute from the Head, as a paragon of all the virtues. He was, we were assured, not only brilliantly clever at his studies, but the best cricketer the School XI had ever fielded, and the best actor the School's dramatic society had ever produced. Both his parents were doctors in the town, and Jack was to have followed in their footsteps, but family troubles multiplied, and he was forced to abandon all hopes of pursuing a medical career. Instead, he settled for the less expensive course of optics, in which he qualified brilliantly, and opened consulting rooms in the town centre. I would drop in there on my way home from teaching in Town School, and often spent hours there in what we both found congenial comradeship. We shared literary ambitions, never fulfilled, and experimented with writing short stories, sometimes in collaboration. But our conversations often turned to the possibility of the expansion of his business, and my joining him in partnership.

In that pre-N.H.S. age he was making a precarious living in a distressed town where the unemployed and their families had no money for such luxuries as eye-testing and spectacles. If their sight was poor they read with magnifying glasses, or with spectacles that could then be purchased at Woolworth's, where you tested your own sight by picking up spectacles from the counter and reading from a test-card.

Opticians are not bound by such stringent rules as doctors, but their association frowns on too blatant advertising, or any touting for business, to the detriment of other opticians. Bartlett fretted and fumed under these restrictions, which frustrated his grandiose schemes, which included the dream of building a sky-scraper tower block. On the ground floor a chiropodist would attend to your feet, and you would then move up the building, until you had your eyes tested on the penultimate floor, and your hair cut at the top of the building. We had many earnest discussions on these lines, and then a young and recently qualified accountant appeared on the scene, and proposed a scheme which captured Jack's imagination. They each put up a nominal sum of money, and launched a company, registered as the 'Optical and Surgical Appliance Benefit Society' (O.S.A.B.S. for short). The company would canvass from door to door, offering spectacles — and later, when a dentist had joined the scheme, dentures — very cheaply and at very low weekly payments. If the canvassers obtained orders they were to recommend the customer to go to Jack for a test. In reality, of course, they could not go anywhere else, as no other optician knew anything of the project. If challenged by the optical association, Jack could truthfully deny that he was canvassing, and explain that these activities were being conducted by a company in which he, Jack, was merely a £1 shareholder.

I was urged to join this get-rich-quick scheme, but I protested that I knew nothing of optics. Jack overcame my objections by offering to teach me, and in a short time I had picked up the rudiments of the art. I soon learned that concave or convex lenses would bend the rays of light reflected from an object, so that its image would fall exactly on the retina of the eye. I was let loose upon the unsuspecting public, a youthful-looking nineteen-year-old, but made to appear more impressive by donning a white coat and dark glasses. (I did not graduate to a white stick and an Alsatian, like the character in Max Boyce's 'incredible plan' to gain admission without a ticket to an international rugby match at Cardiff's National Stadium). I used to operate in a room behind a chemist's shop in Blackwood, to which I travelled several days a week, and I was able to deal with most callers. If I ran into difficulties, such as a case of some optical disease, I would make an appointment for the patient to see "our specialist", Jack, who would visit Blackwood once a week on a mopping-up operation.

I could not exactly overwhelm (I nearly wrote 'blind') callers with science, but I was taught to say, for instance, to some dear old lady with sight problems, that she was "myopic in the oculus dexter", or "hypermetropic in the ocula sinistra": short-sighted in the right eye or long-sighted in the left. One good lady asked me to write it down, so that she could show her husband.

On some days I canvassed for orders or collected the weekly payments, and I suffered some nerve-racking experiences, particularly when the dentist withdrew from the scheme after having extracted teeth from a number of patients.

Irate characters would come to the door in some rough dockland street in Newport, demanding through toothless gums when they might expect their promised dentures, and muttering unintelligible threats. We suffered considerable losses from dishonest canvassers and collectors, one of whom was awaiting trial on a charge of obtaining money by false pretences. One hot summer's day, as I was coming to the end of innumerable canvassing calls, I prepared to repeat for the hundredth time my set-piece formula: "Good afternoon, madam, I represent the Optical and Surgical Appliance Benefit Society, a society to enable you to obtain spectacles and dentures by easy payments." My mind was on the pending trial, as I knew the offender well, and it had been a very hot and tiring day. Making the last call of the afternoon, I mumbled my words, and to my horror heard myself concluding: "... a society to enable you to obtain spectacles and dentures by false pretences."

Another problem was the occasional deaf housewife, especially when she would not come to her front door, but insisted on carrying on a shouted conversation from an upstairs window. My set-piece would be shortened with each repetition, until it was reduced to the single word "Glasses!" When she shouted back "Horses?", I felt it was time to move on to the next door.

The scheme swept the county like a forest fire, and consulting rooms were opened in a number of centres. We were convinced that we were making our fortunes, until the bills for rent, rates, telephones, electricity, etc. came pouring in, and Jack discovered that they exceeded the net takings. His troubles were compounded by the optical association threatening him with investigation, and possible expulsion. Apart from his tottering business, there was a little matter of the irate father of some poor wronged girl threatening to pursue him with a horse-whip. The combination of circumstances proved too much for Jack, and he decided on a strategic withdrawal from Pontypool, for an unknown destination.

His mother was distraught. She called at my home, and begged me to hold the fort, stall the creditors and the irate father, and save her Jack from ruin and disgrace. My own poor mother became even more distraught, and I thought it would be wise if I left home too. Soon I was on my way to London, to seek sanctuary with a kindly aunt. The storm passed, and Jack made a come-back. What happened to the young accountant? Oh, he did rather well, too. He is now a multi-millionaire tycoon of many interests, including insurance and banking.

What other interests enlivened my years in Pontypool? At school in Monmouth I had learned to spell, and so to distinguish between "girls" and "grils". In Pontypool I began to notice the difference between girls and boys, and to exclaim enthusiastically with the French parliamentary backbencher: "Vive la différence!"

My relationship with one girl was strictly platonic, but she introduced a new interest into my life. Muriel taught at Town School, and was a tennis fanatic, with a cannon-ball service, and a forehand and backhand drive like a kick from a mule. She taught me the game, at which I became reasonably proficient, and from which I derived much pleasure in later life, on rare breaks from politics. I still meet her occasionally, with her husband, at the London Welsh rugby club.

A colleague of ours on the staff at Town School shared my interest in law. If the Assizes, which in those days were held in Monmouth, fell during the school holidays, we would go there together in his car, taking with us the girl member of the staff whom he later married, and Muriel. He and I were interested in any case, whatever its nature, but we especially enjoyed cases involving obscure points of law. Whether the two girls shared our enthusiasm, or simply came with us out of loyalty, I never knew. The public gallery would always be packed for a salacious case, but it would empty as soon as that case ended, except for the four faithful musketeers, who always sat it out until the court rose for the day. I never fulfilled my youthful ambition to read law and be called to the bar, but perhaps these Monmouth experiences were of some value in later years, and assisted me in my appearances in witness box or dock, or when prosecuting on the private summonses I took out against interrupters at my meetings.

The chapel was then the centre of much of Welsh life, but it has now weakened its hold. As a boy I accompanied my mother on Sunday evenings, not to the nearest chapel in Pontypool, but to one in neighbouring Pontnewynydd, because a minister we had known in Monmouth was now officiating there. I made my debut on the platform, as every Welsh boy does, singing or reciting — in my case the latter — in the annual school Eisteddfod or chapel 'anniversary'. Max Boyce again has described the scene to perfection, with the small boy in short grey trousers, white shirt and red tie, forgetting his lines, and then being prompted by a row of aunts, mouthing the words like goldfish. I was spared this indignity because I developed a gift for learning poetry rapidly and delivering it with much youthful passion. In a school Eisteddfod I once beat a girl who had been strongly tipped to win the first prize, the second being ear-marked for me. There was no time to switch the labels on the prizes, so I emerged with an ornamental glass cake-stand, and she with a boy's book. The poem to be recited on that occasion was Ode to a Skylark, and I had hailed the blithe spirit with much eloquence.

Each chapel had its youth club, quaintly called a guild, and each arranged its weekly meeting for a different night, so that enthusiasts could do the rounds. They organised debates and ran amateur dramatic societies, both of which appealed to me. Some members, however, preferred lighter entertainment, so a compromise was reached: there would be alternate weeks for debates or plays, and for social evenings, dances, and so on.

Every amateur dramatic society has its tradition of humorous incidents, but I claim first prize for our performance of A. A. Milne's Mr. Wurzel Flummery. Would you believe that a prompter who had attended every rehearsal, and had the script before him on the night, could call out two wrong words in the only three he had to say? He could and he did. Lacking enough members to make up a full cast, we decided that the prompter should take the part of a butler whose sole contribution was to announce a solicitor, a Mr. Denis Clifton. Mr. Clifton duly made his entrance, after being announced in a loud voice from the wings: "Mr. Wurzel Flummery."

Our particular guild in Pontnewynydd was remarkably enterprising, and secured for a nominal rent a private tennis court in Wainfelin, between Pontypool and Pontnewynydd. We used to play on every possible summer evening, and at weekends. My summer holidays were now fully occupied; it was tennis from dawn to dusk, six days a week. In the South Wales of the thirties no one would have dared to play on Sundays.

What other memories do I retain of the years before I became of age in 1936? A toe on my left foot developed into a most peculiar shape, and my doctor took one quick look at it and pronounced an instant verdict: "Have it off!" The amputation was performed in Pontypool Hospital, and in the subsequent weeks I became the object of much attention as I hopped up and down my street on crutches. I invented a game of seeing how far I could get in one hop, stretching the crutches out ahead of me to their full extent and then taking a giant's step. I would usually reach the other side of the road in one, unless the crutches slipped, as they frequently did. I also enlivened the monotony of convalescence without sport by inflicting on any poor unsuspecting girl who might be prepared to listen that old, old chestnut: "Would you like to see the place where I had my operation?" If she showed any interest, I would point out to her the hospital on the hill across the valley.

I used to save industriously from my earnings from coaching, so that I could have an annual fortnight's holiday in London, where I used to stay in Kilburn, near to an uncle who lived in that area. During the hours when he was at work I explored London, concentrating on all the free or low-priced places of interest, thereby stretching my meagre savings so as to last out the fourteen days. I became an authority on London's museums, art galleries, and parks, having walked for miles in search of them. I survived on lunches of the cheapest salads, washed down with a glass of water, and I came to know London better than many born and bred there.

I have already explained how my 1934 holiday introduced me to the British Union of Fascists, and of my joining the movement in March 1935. This further antagonised my father; my mother was sympathetic at first, but she hated arguments and family dissensions, the flames of which were now being fanned. In the summer of 1936 I packed a suitcase and left Pontypool for London, to begin a new chapter in my life. At first I returned every holiday, but then at less frequent intervals as old friends moved away from the town, and my ties with it were gradually loosened. But I have continued to make the occasional visit, and I retain the fondest and happiest memories of my youth there.

Chapter Six

"This won't do the school any good. I'll have to make other arrangements. I'll see the agents about it." These three sentences became catch-phrases in the private school where I returned to teaching. The first was the Head's complaint about some misdemeanour, real or imagined, on the part of one of his staff. The second was a thinly veiled threat to sack the offender. The third affirmed his intention of applying to a scholastic agency in search of a replacement for the unfortunate victim of his displeasure. Evelyn Waugh said it first and said it all in his Decline and Fall. But surely he exaggerated the absurdities of our private schools? Not at all, as anyone who has shared my experiences, especially in the nineteen thirties, can confirm.

I started looking for work as soon as I arrived in London from Pontypool, and I first found employment in an off-licence at Muswell Hill. But my aunt thought it sad for me to throw away my years of experience as a student-teacher, and a friend advised me to consult the scholastic agents Truman and Knightley, then in Conduit Street. Waugh has expertly described the grading of vacancies for teachers in private schools under the triple headings of 'first-class school', 'second-class school', and 'school'. Uncannily accurate is his description of an interview at a 'school', where the attractive and reasonably well paid position notified to the agency is, alas, no longer vacant, or it might be that your qualifications were not quite suited. Of course, one would be told, there is a junior position available, at a much lower salary, which might perhaps interest you. In the crisis years of the thirties it would and it did.

The agency told me of a vacancy at Lewes Grammar School, a foundation with a very fine reputation. But alas again, the vacancy proved to be at another school of the same name, a small private school at the top of the steep and winding Lewes High Street on the way from the centre of the town to the prison and the old race-course. I telephoned and was told that the Head, the Reverend Cecil Lewis, was on his way to London, and would be arriving at Victoria Station at a certain time. I dashed up to Victoria, recognised the cleric from the description I had been given, introduced myself, and began to talk him into offering me the post. I succeeded in breaking down any reluctance aroused by this unorthodox approach; he offered me the post, and I accepted.

At this school every member of the teaching staff other than graduates (if any) was required to wear an undergraduate academic gown, so as to impress the parents who sent their unfortunate offspring to educational establishments along the south coast which attracted their victims by charging high fees and adopting even higher-sounding names. Many a poor boy suffered in these Dotheboys Halls, which rejoiced in such grandiose titles as 'Buckingham College'. I went to the Information Desk which was then a special attraction at Selfridges, where the staff could answer immediately all manner of questions, such as which horse had won the Derby in 1892. My own question was more practical: where could I buy an undergraduate's gown? At Ede and Ravenscroft's, in Chancery Lane, came the answer, given without a moment's hesitation. I hurried off there and bought my gown, together with the formal pin-stripe black suit which the Head demanded for Sunday wear: a metamorphosis from the white coat and dark glasses of my Optical and Surgical Appliance days.

School terms begin in mid-September, and it was always my fate to arrive on or close to my birthday, for the beginning of the new scholastic year. In mid-September 1936 I took the train from Victoria to Lewes, and climbed the hill. I was soon to appreciate the joke which told how one new member of the staff had asked a passerby the way to the school, and misunderstood the directions. In error he had gone to the prison, and had been there a week before he discovered his mistake.

What were the staff's grievances? First of all, poor pay, which was common to all such establishments. My salary was £50 a year, plus bed and board. (Another school joke asked which was the bed and which the board). National insurance contributions were deducted from the cheque handed to us at the end of each term, and in my case this reduced the sum coming to me to something between £15 and £16. If I had returned for a second year I would have been forced to survive some seven or eight weeks of holidays, plus the following term, until I received a cheque for a similar amount at Christmas.

Did the bed and board compensate for the lack of money? The bed was perhaps not as uncomfortable as the joke implied, but the board was not clearly discernable to the naked eye. Dinner each evening was a particularly sick joke. We would sit in our staff room on the first floor, the pangs of hunger gnawing at us as the hours passed since our meagre lunch, impatiently waiting for the gong which would summon us to the feast. At last it would ring out, loud and clear, a clarion call which would have awakened the dead, or the fox from his lair in the morning. Down the stairs we would troop, and into the dining-room — to a sumptuous repast of bread, cheese, and water.

The slices of bread were strictly rationed; the piece of cheese was minute: but the water was plentiful, with a jug filled to the brim. The Head's wife and daughter went through the motions of dining with us, and one or other would politely ask if we wanted more water, and would be ready and willing to take the jug to the kitchen to replenish it. We were certain that they later joined the Head in an ample meal, denied to us.

Every subterfuge was adopted to coax extra rations from the cook, or from her assistant, the Head's daughter. This gave rise to a school song which included the words: "If you're not in love with the Headmaster's daughter, then you can't have a second piece of cake!"

Chapter Six

We could not afford to eat out. Sometimes I would walk the streets, and stop longingly outside a shop, jingling the few pence in my pocket, and gazing through the window like the Bisto kids in the advertisements of the period, trying to decide whether to throw all discretion to the winds and invest in a bar of chocolate. We scoured the local newspapers for news of public functions at which 'light refreshments are provided free': we were ardent members of the Y.M.C.A[1], and any other society offering this attractive bait.

Lack of money and of food were not our only complaints. The Head was an extraordinary character, the personification of all the idiosyncrasies of mankind, many of which I had never encountered before. One of his tricks was to start a conversation in what appeared to be its middle, thus leaving one to guess at its subject matter. We dared not ask questions, for fear of being abused as idiots, and threatened with the opening sentences of this chapter.

An example springs to mind. The Head addressed me one afternoon, as I sat alone in the staff room, with the words: "They're on the premises!" What or who might be on the premises? Housebreakers? The bailiffs? These and other likely and unlikely answers raced through my brain, all to be discarded. I played for time, while he pressed me with the leading question: "Well, what are you going to do about it?" This was a difficult one to answer, with no knowledge of the identity of the visitors. I stalled again, with the polite inquiry: "What would you suggest I did?"

After much manoeuvring and mental circling and sparring around this difficult opponent, the lead I was seeking was forthcoming. By deduction worthy of a Sherlock Holmes I came to the conclusion that the visiting cricket team had arrived

---

[1]   It was in the Lewes Y.M.C.A. that I listened to the abdication speech of King Edward VIII, later a neighbour and friend of the Mosleys. I never met him, but once spoke to him on the telephone.

from another school, and that I should have been downstairs to welcome them. I survived this and other such ordeals, and emerged with sharpened faculties.

The Head was an uncouth man, with no thought of knocking on classroom doors, which he would throw open without warning. Without a word of apology he would interrupt the lesson in progress, halting the unfortunate teacher in mid-sentence while he questioned a boy about some alleged misdemeanour. He was always in hot pursuit of money the boys owed him for books supplied, and one incident became a classic in the school's legends. A young and enthusiastic history teacher was holding his class enthralled with a graphic description of the Romans landing in Britain on their first invasion. Even the bravest legionaries paled and hesitated when they saw the fierce Britons, painted with woad, lining the shore, until the standard-bearer raised aloft the Roman eagle, jumped into the shallow water, and waded towards the shore, crying ... At this point the door was flung open, an angry figure appeared, an accusing finger was pointed at an unhappy boy, and a booming voice completed the interrupted sentence: "You owe me three and four pence!"

At the end of a harrowing day our spirits would be revived by one senior master whose sense of humour never deserted him. Mr. Pope would stagger up the stairs to the staff room and collapse in a chair. "What sort of a day have you had?", we would solicitously inquire. "Not bad, not bad", would be the reply. "Only fourteen snubs and seventeen insults!" He delighted in outrageously teasing a Head whose ignorance of English literature, and even of the most common proverbial sayings, was incredible. He would listen with feigned sympathy to the Head's latest tale of woe, and then murmur some comment like: "Well, sir, you know the old saying: 'It's a long worm that has no turning.'" Even our Head entertained some doubt as to the accuracy of this observation, but he lacked the confidence to challenge the ebullient Mr. Pope. Instead he would mutter: "Is it really, Mr. Pope? Yes, I suppose it is."

Chapter Six

The Head said Grace before and after meals with the boys; when he was absent Mr. Pope, as senior master, would deputise. With lowered head, closed eyes, and hands piously folded he would murmur, just loud enough for the nearest boys to hear without being quite sure that they had heard correctly. His Grace before meat was: "For what we are about to receive, may the Lord have mercy upon us." After the meal his benediction ran: "For what we might have received, may the Lord make us truly thankful."

Our reverend persecutor had posted on the staff-room wall a list of rules and regulations for the staff; beneath them, heavily underlined in red, was the stern injunction: "The observance of these rules will avoid unpleasantness." On one occasion Mr. Pope entertained us with an apocryphal tale, which he illustrated with a wealth of gesture. He claimed to have been hurrying from the staff-room to the stairs which led below when he became aware of the Head running after him. He ran down the stairs, along the hall, and up a parallel flight of stairs. Looking over his shoulder and noticing that the Head was still in pursuit, he ran down the first flight and again along the hall. "What on earth do you think you are doing, Mr. Pope?" bellowed the Head. "I'm avoiding unpleasantness, sir!" was the alleged reply.

Our duties were not confined to the classroom, but extended to awakening the boys and seeing that they were bathed, dressed and downstairs in time for breakfast, the process being reversed at night. On Sunday mornings we escorted them to and from church, and during the week to their games of football on the Downs above Lewes. The boys loved to hear me talk about rugby, and were forever pestering me to show them how it was played. This was strictly against the rules, whose observance would avoid unpleasantness, but one day they wore down my resistance. I gave a ball to a big, well-built boy of about sixteen, and told him to run with it, so that I could tackle him. I did so, and he fell down. As he lay on the ground laughing, with the other boys crowded round, he worked one leg free and was kicking with it in the air, for fun. His boot caught me just above my left eye, and opened up a wide and deep wound. There ensued one of those grotesque performances which could surely have occurred nowhere except at Lewes Grammar School. What should I have done next? Obviously I should have hurried back to the school for first-aid, before having the wound stitched. But this would have provoked an absurd interview with the Head, who would have accused the poor boy of having kicked me deliberately. Severe punishment would have followed. So a council of war was hastily summoned, and all the boys were called upon to take the most solemn oath of secrecy as to what had really happened. All were pledged to support my somewhat unlikely story that I had collided with a goal-post. The Head believed us, and all was well, except that I foolishly neglected to have the wound stitched, so that in healing it pulled my left eyebrow downwards. This was the first of many accidents which gradually destroyed what little natural beauty I might have had at birth.

The conspiratorial relationship between staff and boys of which this incident was typical, made life bearable. It was the only feasible relationship on which discipline could have been maintained. A boy in search of the Head would ask one of the staff: "Have you seen the old pot and pan anywhere, sir?" How could you reprimand the boy when this piece of rhyming slang was such an apt description of "the Old Man"? Lewes was then a racing town, and the boys tended to be the sons of owners, trainers, or jockeys, full of fun and that zest for life which is the hallmark of the world of sport. I remember them with affection.

My duties left me little time for active politics, and I recall going to only one Blackshirt meeting during my year at Lewes. It was a particularly noisy one on the Level, at Brighton. The speaker, the late Tommy Moran, of naval boxing fame, was to become a dear friend in later years. The 'Red Front' was present in considerable force, with the comrades chanting a parody of a popular song of the day, "Bye-bye, Blackbird". As they surged around the loudspeaker van their voices rose:

Chapter Six

"You can take your Union Jack, Go to hell and don't come back: Blackshirts, bye-bye."

They succeeded in cutting the wires leading to the loudspeaker, but Tommy possessed a powerful pair of lungs, as well as enormous physical courage, and he succeeded in making himself heard above the din, as he continued to propagate British Union policies. After the meeting I fell in with the local Blackshirts and marched with them back to their headquarters, near Brighton station.

In mid-July 1937 I left Lewes Grammar School, ostensibly for my summer holidays, but in reality with no intention of returning in September if I could find an alternative post. Almost as soon as I reached London I saw one advertised, at a private school in Harrow. It proved an infinite improvement on Lewes, although it did not quite deserve its grandiloquent name of 'The King's School', for it consisted merely of two houses in St. John's Road. I was interviewed and accepted, my duties to begin in mid-September.

I stayed in London until the end of July. August took me on one of the most memorable holidays of my life, the fulfilment of a boyhood ambition, though not in the form or in the country that I had originally desired. In my Pontypool schooldays French had been one of my favourite subjects. I had fallen in love with the French language from my first halting steps in it at the little school in Monmouth, and it is a first love to which I have remained faithful. It has, in fact, grown stronger over the years, as I have gained a deeper knowledge of the language, the country and its people.

At school in Pontypool French pen-friends were much encouraged, and I corresponded for years with a boy called Robert Mestat, who lived in Macon. Then someone introduced into the school the idea of corresponding with French girls, and this naturally became popular. From somewhere I obtained the address of one Marguerite Parcellier, whose name I recall more clearly than that of her home town, which was somewhere in the Bordeaux area. Nor can I recall how I progressed from her to a Corsican girl, in Bastia, with the somewhat striking name of Lulu Graziani. In letters to all three pen-friends I dropped thinly-veiled hints that I would love to spend a holiday in their beautiful home-towns. I was particularly eloquent in singing the praises of Corsica, Vile de beaute, but to no avail. Neither Lulu nor her parents rose to the bait. I could not afford to pay for a holiday in France, nor anywhere else abroad, and I had to wait until 1939 before I paid my first visit to France.

But my politics had opened up other possibilities. British Union's journal The Blackshirt carried advertisements from time to time from continental boys and girls who wished to correspond with members of our movement. I replied to such an advertisement from a Dutch girl, although I appreciated that our correspondence would have to be conducted entirely in English, as I knew no Dutch. After writing my first letter, I watched the postman for a reply, but none came. Weeks and months passed, and then came a note from her to say that she had been showered with letters, from which she had picked at random one name and address, which was not mine. She had, however, passed my name and address, and those of two other young men, to three German girls of her acquaintance. They all lived in Heidelberg, and they all shared the name Gertrud. In due course I received a letter from Gertrud Fritz. Later I was to meet her namesakes of the Welschinger and Schneider families.

Gertrud Fritz and I corresponded regularly for some time, and my hints that I would like to visit Germany became ever broader, until at last I wore down all resistance. Her mother — she had no father — gave permission for Gertrud to ask me if I would care to holiday with them. Would I? No doubt I replied that I could not possibly consider imposing on them in that way, but how kind of them, and if they insisted . . . They did, and off I went, on or about the first day of August 1937, returning on the last day of the month, after four full and unforgettable weeks.

Chapter Six

I travelled by train from Victoria to Dover, and from there by boat to Ostend, where I took a continental express which crossed the frontier into Germany near Aachen. My impressions of that journey are still vivid. Belgium was not then the scrupulously clean country it became later. Its railway stations were unattractive, and the porters seemed always to be lounging against the pillars of the stations, or else leaning on their barrows. Then the train crossed the frontier, and I was in a new world. The first German station that I saw was spotless, and the porters looked like guardsmen on parade. This and subsequent impressions were not caused by my looking at National Socialist Germany through rose-tinted — or should it be black-tinted? — spectacles of a British Fascist.

On my return journey a month later the train was packed with ordinary British holiday-makers, unanimous in praise of what they had seen. Only later did this become unfashionable, so that everything in Germany had to be denigrated. It was in that later period that I heard someone assuring his audience that the Rhine was a dirty, foul-smelling river!

Through the window of the train I drank in the beauty of the German countryside, down the winding Rhine from Koln to Mannheim, past the Lorelei rock and the fairy castles perched high on cliffs which rose sheer from the glittering water. But my eye was political and economic as well as romantic, and I observed with interest how every available square inch of land was cultivated along the railway embankments, almost up to the rails, in Germany's effort to be self-sufficient, and so independent of international finance.

At Mannheim I changed, and took a local train up the valley of the Neckar, on which Heidelberg stands. Gertrud was waiting for me, with her friends, as I stepped off the train and into the station booking-hall. Across the station ran an enormous banner in red and black, adorned with the swastika emblem, bearing the legend: " Die deutsche Grüsse — Heil Hitler!" I was welcomed with this greeting, and a salute. The greeting I was to hear every day, and many times a day, throughout my stay. They were the first words I heard of a morning, as I came from my bedroom into the dining-room, before my hosts asked me if I had slept well. They were the last words I heard at night, after they had wished me a good night's sleep. I can hear them now: "Heil Hitler. Haben Sie gut geschlafen?" in the morning, and " Gute Nacht. Schlafen Sie gut. Heil Hitler", at night.

My hosts showed me all the tourist sights: the old student inns where generations of young men and women from all over the world had written or carved their names on the walls, ceilings, and blackened oak beams of the beer cellars. During my stay I tried desperately to pay for entertainment when I was out with the girls, but Gertrud insisted that this was not a German custom. I was her guest, and no German hostess could possibly allow her guest to pay for anything. I would insist, and slip money into her pocket, but only to find it under my pillow at night.

I was taken to a magnificent performance of Romeo and Juliet in the courtyard of the old castle, where stood the famous beer barrel which the dwarf Perkeo was alleged to have drunk dry in a single night. I was driven to Stuttgart along an early autobahn, many years before Britain built its first motorway. My hosts asked me to tell them things that I would like to see, or to say if I would prefer to go out alone and see things for myself. Germany, they insisted, had nothing to hide. In so far as time and opportunity allowed, I saw it all. In retrospect I certainly would not praise, or even condone everything, such as the notices over the doors of restaurants and places of entertainment: Juden sind hier unerwunscht — Jews not wanted here. Or the more stark: Juden sind hier streng verboten — Jews strictly forbidden here. All this has been discussed too often for further analysis in this brief story, but let me display an honesty often sadly lacking in many who admired Germany in that era, but now pretend that they had always opposed it. I saw it all, and most of what I saw I liked.

Chapter Six

There were some other blemishes, and at times even my hosts, ardent supporters of the Nazi Party, were embarrassed. Especially they disliked the crude obscenities of Streicher's newspaper Der Stunner, and Rosenberg's anti-Christian campaign. But I treasure a host of happier memories of that holiday. In my native South Wales I had been used to high unemployment and the depressing sight of men without hope, rotting away on street corners. Germany had twice the number of unemployed that we had in Britain. Until full employment could be achieved the unemployed were drafted into the Arbeitsdienst, the labour service in which every man of sound health was obliged to serve for six months, with no distinction of class. I often watched them marching back to camp after their hard day of manual labour. They carried their picks and shovels on their shoulders, and these tools, which had restored to their bearers the dignity of labour, were burnished and shone in the afternoon sun, as they marched with the precision of the Brigade of Guards.

Equally with their fellows in employment, they enjoyed every facility for sport and recreation, from football to opera, either free or for a nominal payment, upon production of their membership card of the Kraft durch Freude (Strength through Joy) organisation. Was there nothing in this from which Britain might have learned? Or was it really all evil, designed for war and world conquest?

In later, post-war years I endorsed Mosley's condemnation of German wartime atrocities, refusing to be drawn into a silly numbers game as to exactly how many victims were involved, because it is always wrong to inflict death or torture on any helpless prisoner. Have former communists who for so long sang the praises of Stalinist Russia ever made a comparable condemnation of their erstwhile hero, 'Uncle Joe'?

There is no virtue in exchanging atrocity stories, assessing the degrees of wickedness of this or that notorious murderer. But can it be denied, as a simple historical fact, that Stalin murdered infinitely more people in the cold blood of peace than Hitler did in the hot blood of war?

My relationship with my friend Gertrud was platonic, or only mildly romantic, but the charm of Old Heidelberg swept me off my feet. Since that time I have often quoted, with feeling, the famous lines beginning: "Ich hab'mein Herz in Heidelberg verloren ..." Two weeks after my return to London I presented myself at the King's School, Harrow, on my twenty-second birthday, to begin on the following day my first term in a new school and a new chapter in my life.

Chapter Seven

"What has happened to the King's School spirit?" my new Head used to ask, the question being rhetorical, as the boys at early morning assembly were not expected to break silence and reply. The Head was an Anglican clergyman of uncertain position on the rungs of the ladder leading from Low Church to High Church. He liked to be addressed as Father Warburton, but was prone to denounce other clergymen as 'Anglo-Catholic puppies'.

His entry into holy orders was the subject of an amusing anecdote. In his youth he had been a teacher in a State school, where his proclaimed Anglicanism had resulted in more than one brush with authority. On one occasion he had departed from the non-sectarian syllabus and given his class a lesson on the meaning of All Saints' Day. This produced an angry letter of protest from the Baptist father of one of the boys. "Sir", his letter began, "my church doesn't believe in saints." The young Warburton had poured oil on troubled flames by replying: "Sir, the saints don't believe in your church." There had been an angry scene with the headmaster and the boy's father, and Warburton decided to leave the school and enter the church. After his ordination he had served for a while as a missionary-teacher in Lagos, but was now head of his own private school in Harrow.

This alleged lack of school spirit was the subject of much ribaldry among the staff. At that time Worthington's were running a series of advertisements based on the particular room in their houses where their customers stored their beer, and one advertisement read: 'At No. 17 they keep it under the stairs.' The school occupied numbers 17 and 19 in the road, so we could not resist suggesting that perhaps the spirit had disappeared in that direction.

Chapter Seven

Father Warburton had been twice married, and had fathered a daughter, Grace, by his first wife, and another daughter, Jean, by his second. Grace was fanatically devoted to her father, and used to take offence at even our mildest criticisms of him, including the rather feeble joke about the school spirit. She became particularly angry one day when one of us suggested that a notice outside the school had been placed there deliberately, as a reflection on the manner in which the school was conducted. The council roadmen were at work, and a section of the road had been raised above the normal level. Motorists were warned of this by a notice which read: "Beware of the ramp". Grace thought this not at all funny.

By this time I was a political zealot. With the ingenuousness of my twenty-two years I had affirmed my support for the policies of Sir Oswald Mosley and his British Union movement within half an hour of entering the staff-room for the first time. The staff, whether sympathetic to my views or not, were unanimous in advising me to conceal them from the Head, who was strongly anti-fascist. This put me in an awkward position, because on my arrival I had somehow been manoeuvred into the place next to the Head in the dining room, which we shared with him and his family. My colleagues had all become thoroughly bored with the Head's tedious pontificating, and no one wanted to occupy the place next to him, which meant bearing the full brunt of his tirades, and making appropriate or inappropriate comments when he paused for breath, as he did very occasionally. Perhaps I found it easier to converse with him, or at least to give a semblance of attention, than some had done. At any rate, towards the end of a meal, if the Head and I were well launched into a discussion, the rest of the staff, and the family, would murmur their excuses, rise from the table, and quietly tip-toe from the room, leaving me alone with the lion in his den.

Politics were frequently the subject of discussion, and I would parry all references to Mosley and British Union with vague suggestions that I 'believed' they said this or that, or that I 'thought' they said something else. All went well until one fateful day when, by a most unfortunate slip of the tongue, I said 'we say' instead of 'they say'. Cats of every shape and colour slipped out of bags, and much fat flew into the fire. There was a furious argument, but unlike my previous employer Father Warburton did not talk of 'making other arrangements.' Instead, he politely inquired whether I might not be happier in another school.

To leave so soon after my arrival would not have suited my plans at all, so I parried with a warm assurance that I was supremely happy where I was. The mental sparring continued for some time, but I stuck to my guns, and eventually weathered the storm. He was kind enough to say that he considered me a good teacher, and did not want to lose me from his staff. This was an improvement on the comment of the headmaster at Lewes, who had once informed me that he thought I might make a good teacher — "in about fifty years." The arguments between Father Warburton and me continued, but there was an undercurrent of friendship and mutual respect between us, and before I left I spent a Christmas with him and his family, as his guest.

Every private school has a quota of eccentrics on its staff, and the King's School was no exception. One day Father Warburton produced a semi-literate letter from a young man asking if he might be given temporary employment, so that he might benefit from the assistance of the Head in his theological studies.

Moved by Christian charity, and the wish to help a future ordinand, and with an eye also perhaps on the opportunity to secure cheap labour, Father Warburton invited the young man to join the staff as a junior French master. His name was Warner, so he inevitably became 'Plum', after the famous Kent cricketer of the period.

It was soon apparent that he knew practically no French at all, but he bluffed his way through junior classes by keeping one page ahead of the boys, who used to complain to other masters that if they asked how to pronounce a French word they were told to "look it up". On one occasion there was to be a football match between staff and boys, and a master with a classical bent had written a Latin tag — from Vergil — below a list of the teams' names pinned up on the school notice-board: Parcere subjectis et debellare superbos — Spare the vanquished, and down with the proud.

We persuaded Plum that this quotation was in French, and asked him, as an expert in the language, to translate it for us less gifted mortals. He professed to understand it all (though without vouchsafing a translation) except for the last word, and he was greatly teased over his ignorance of this "well known French word" superbos. We gave it an appropriate French pronunciation and a wealth of Gallic gesture. We were rather cruel to poor Plum.

Another member of the staff had what seemed to be the most Cockney accent that could ever have moved beyond the sound of Bow Bells. For some obscure reason he had been put in charge of the Literary and Debating Society. We used to listen, with fatal fascination, for his announcement: "There will be a mee'ing of the Li'erary and Deba'ing Socie'y in the School 'all ar'er school." On one school Prize Day Father Warburton was thrilled to have as guest speaker the then Bishop of London, Dr. Winnington-Ingram. During his address the Bishop had referred to life as "like a bird, flying through a storm, buffeted by wind and rain, seeing a light and flying towards it. The light was in a room with an open window and the bird had flown in, to be warmed and refreshed, before resuming its flight." As soon as the Bishop had departed Father Warburton rushed into the staff-room, in a state of wild excitement. "We must report the Bishop's speech in the school magazine. Who can remember its main points?" There was a long silence. Then a little Cockney voice piped up: "Som'at abaht a bird flyin 'abaht, wasn't it?"

Life in the school at Harrow was a huge improvement on that at Lewes, while the slightly higher salary and proximity to London helped to make our social life more agreeable. For some time I clung to my belief that England had produced in Shakespeare its only dramatist, and my theatre-going was confined to the Open Air Theatre in Regents Park. I had attended a performance there in its opening year, and except for the war years have scarcely missed a production since.

Of recent years the company has extended its repertoire, but A Midsummer Night's Dream is still almost an annual event. It is so perfectly suited to performance on a balmy summer night, notwithstanding the distractions caused by birds twittering in the trees, or low-flying aircraft, often the subject of comment from the critics in the next day's papers. Even under these conditions the Dream remains magic to its devotees, of whom I am one.

I once attended a performance in the company of a Harrow colleague, a Mackay from the Wirral. He was a man of many parts, a brilliant tennis player, a jovial companion, but also a serious lover of the classics. Conversation with him, at any level, serious or frivolous, was a delight. On this occasion we fell into conversation with two girls, one of whom opened my eyes to a much wider vista of the world of the theatre.

Doris came from Islington, and had left school at the earliest leaving age, to enter the Civil Service. But she had read widely, and had developed a range of artistic interests. She was secretary to the Sadlers Wells Circle, a sort of supporters' club for the famous Rosebery Avenue theatre. She introduced me to ballet and opera, breaking me in gently with the lightest of these, and leading me on gradually to the more serious. I owe her a great debt of gratitude for opening to me a world which, but for that chance meeting, I might have ignored. Together we saw practically every West End theatre production between the summer of 1938 and the outbreak of war, when the theatres began to close.

Since joining British Union in March 1935 I had been a Headquarters Member, i.e. one not attached to any branch, but my membership was now transferred to Harrow Branch, a particularly thriving one, since it lay in Mosley's first parliamentary constituency. It was from Harrow that he had entered Parliament, as a twenty-two year old Conservative, and it was there that he was later returned as an Independent, after he had left the Conservative Party. Many local shopkeepers still remembered him from those days. I recall in particular a newsagent telling me that if Mosley ever returned and offered himself again as a candidate, under whatever label, he would be assured of his vote.

I am always pleased that I joined British Union before I heard Mosley speak. I was not brought into the movement under the spell of his oratory or his personal magnetism, but simply through reading his policies and thinking that they were right. There were too many 'Albert Hall fascists', swept into the movement on a wave of excitement at some monster rally, only to weaken when they found themselves in more isolated situations and subject to abuse, with no friendly crowds around them.

I first heard Mosley speak at a monster meeting in Limehouse, in East London, and the impression he made on me confirmed me in my convictions. I am deeply moved by great pieces of music, but perhaps I am even more stirred by the spoken word. Mosley was probably the greatest orator of this century, certainly in my opinion vastly superior to Churchill. Mosley himself considered that he was possibly inferior to Lloyd George, that other great spellbinder and spinner of words.

I did not get to know Mosley personally until after the second World War, so I will postpone my personal impressions of him to a later chapter, but his pre-war speeches inspired me, and oft-quoted phrases are as fresh now as when I first heard them. "We have lit a flame that will never be extinguished. Guard that flame until it illumines Britain, and lights again the path of mankind." Or on another occasion: "We care not whether we win tomorrow morning, or at the end of a lifetime of struggle, but win we will because Britain demands it, and nothing can hold down the spirit of Britain reborn." He did not live to see that victory, and I have not lived long enough to see it, but that message remains for me a deep all-abiding truth.

Now, while I was teaching in Harrow, Mosley came to speak at a hall in nearby Kenton, and at the end of the meeting he spoke to me briefly, and I shook his hand for the first time. An incident from that meeting has remained in my memory because it illustrated his skill in handling hecklers, making nonsense of the allegation that they were brutally set upon at his meetings, and ejected with unnecessary force.

A group of students sitting in a row close to the platform kept up a steady flow of insults throughout the speech. Mosley ignored them completely. Then came question time. I watched the students consulting together, evidently preparing a question designed to render Mosley speechless. At last one of them rose, with the nonchalance of an Oxford or Cambridge undergraduate of the thirties, flung his scarf a further twirl round his neck, took his pipe out of his mouth, and in an affected drawl asked: "I say, Mosley, what is your movement's attitude towards birth control?" Much tittering and applause from the daring young man's companions. Mosley drew himself up to his full height, hands on hips, and looked the young man up and down, before replying: "After looking at you, I should think the question of birth control comes about twenty years too late. Next question, please." The questioner subsided into his seat, and the meeting continued to a triumphant conclusion. There were no further interruptions.

By the time I joined the movement I was already well versed in its policies, so that within a few months I won two out of three essay competitions open to readers of The Blackshirt. The issue of 15 August 1935 reported: 'The winner of the last Essay Competition for readers of The Blackshirt is E.J. Hamm, Pontypool, Mon. The subject of the essay was The Occupational

Franchise, and Mr. Hamm's essay was obviously the best submitted. It will be remembered that this member also won the competition on The Movement's India Policy.'

Because of the disapproval of the headmaster of my school I could not play as active a political role locally as I would have liked, but I took part in marches in central and east London, and stewarded a number of meetings outside London. In Harrow I felt it best to confine myself to writing letters, under a nom-de-plume, to the Harrow Observer, and also to the Pontypool Free Press at home. One of my letters to the latter paper produced a reply, also written under a nom de plume. When I discovered the identity of my fellow-correspondent I was surprised. Edna was a Pontypool girl I knew well by sight, and to whom I had spoken casually as she was a friend of the Minsons, for whom I had worked as an errand boy. (Mr. Minson later joined British Union). I knew nothing of her politics, and was astonished to find that she and her friend Gwyn, both teachers, were members of British Union. Edna's father was secretary of a local grocers' association, and I accompanied her once when she was delivering letters for him.

We called at a small grocer's shop, off the beaten track in a remote part of the Eastern Valley of Monmouthshire. After delivering her letter to the proprietor Edna said: "You should read this", and handed him a copy of Action (the new British Union journal). "I do", he replied, producing a copy from under the counter. There has been much wild guessing as to the membership figures of British Union, which were deliberately kept secret, but our opponents always underestimated their strength. This little incident is indicative of the widespread latent support that the movement enjoyed among people who were not formally members.

Among the London marches in which I took part was that from Kentish Town to Trafalgar Square in July 1938, and one from the Embankment to Bermondsey in October of the same year. We always marched in perfect order, in spite of the provocative shouting of obscenities from the mob which shuffled and shambled alongside us. We were surely entitled to march anywhere, but our marches through East London have often been criticised on the grounds that they were a deliberate provocation of the Jewish community. This is quite untrue. Mosley was very popular in East London, and his movement had a large and enthusiastic following there. We had no quarrel with any immigrant minority, ordinary people in no way concerned with the machinations of that international finance which was our real target. If they had not been stirred up by agitators from outside there would have been little or no trouble. This was the situation in such British Union strongholds as Bethnal Green and Shoreditch. We never marched in Whitechapel, where we had no support, and where our meetings might reasonably have been construed as provocative.

I was not at the famous Olympia meeting of 7 June 1934, of which such a gory legend persists. In his book The Fascists in Britain, published in 1961, Colin Cross speaks of a 'prepared Fascist drill', whereby at each catcall from the audience Mosley would stop speaking, and spotlights on the platform would be focussed on the interrupter, who would then be violently set upon. In fact, Mosley stopped speaking only when the loud-speaker wires had been temporarily severed by Communists, thousands of whom had marched to Olympia, armed with offensive weapons, against which Blackshirt stewards retaliated with their bare hands only. As to the 'searchlights', these belonged to the newsreel companies, and were not under British Union control at all.

Documentary evidence can be produced to substantiate the above, but let me quote direct from one distinguished observer at the meeting. In the Sunday Pictorial of 24 June 1934 Lloyd George commented: 'Personally I have suffered as much as anyone in public life today from hostile interruptions by opponents determined to make it impossible for me to put my case before audiences. Naturally, therefore, I have an antipathy to that class of interruption, and I feel that men who enter meetings with the deliberate intention of suppressing free speech have no right to complain if an exasperated audience handles them rudely.' Professor Robert Skidelsky, who can hardly be accused of partiality, says in his biography Oswald Mosley, published in 1975, that altogether only about fifty people were ejected from the Olympia meeting, and that although a number of people, including British Union members, were treated in nearby hospitals, one only was detained for more than a short time. Three weeks later this anti-Fascist was fit and well again, in active opposition, and showing no sign of injury.

Of these great London rallies my most unforgettable memories are of the meeting at Earls Court on 16 July 1939, the largest indoor meeting held anywhere in the world. Some thirty thousand people packed the vast hall to hear Mosley make an impassioned plea for peace, as the dark clouds of war gathered overhead. An unkindly reference to Winston Churchill brought a storm of prolonged applause, but prompted a figure seated in the front row to rise and leave the hall. It was Churchill's son Randolph. At this meeting and at all others after Olympia there was perfect order. The power of Red Front violence had been broken, and freedom of speech had been restored in Britain.

I spent part of August 1939 at home in Pontypool, but before the end of the month I had returned to London. From then on I took part in all the demonstrations organised by British Union to try to avert the tragedy of war. On the Wednesday evening before war was declared I was in the vast crowd packing St. Martin's Lane when Mosley called for a show of hands on the issue of peace or war. He had coined the slogan: "Let the people vote !" and demanded a national referendum, but the government would have none of it. They had been elected in 1935 on a peace programme, but were now intent on war, without consulting the people in any way. So at the St. Martin's Lane meeting, and at many others, Mosley put it to the vote. A forest of arms would be raised for peace; a handful only for war. These meetings went off with no disturbance, no harassment of any kind from any quarter.

On the morning of Sunday, 3 September 1939, when staying with relatives in North London, I was preparing to go to Bethnal Green, where Mosley was to speak at an open-air meeting. Over the radio came the news that the meeting had been banned, on the pretext that an air raid might be imminent. Then came the sound of Big Ben chiming out eleven o'clock. After a pause, there came the sombre voice of the Prime Minister, Neville Chamberlain, informing us that Britain was at war with Germany. A jumble of confused and angry thoughts flooded my mind, among them memories of my holiday in Germany. How could I fight against my friends in Heidelberg? How could I try to kill them? Suppose I became a bomber pilot and was called upon to bomb that beautiful university city? Yet I could not have refused. I had always rejected pacifism, even in my most ardent League of Nations days. Striving for peace, I had always known that if my country were attacked I would fight to defend it.

On 1 September, Mosley had issued certain instructions to all members of British Union, while at the same time exercising his legal and democratic right to carry on his campaign of public meetings in favour of peace. This right had been exercised during previous wars by such distinguished public figures as William Pitt the Elder, Edmund Burke, Charles James Fox, Cobden and Bright, Joseph Chamberlain, Gladstone, Lloyd George, and Ramsay McDonald. Even while hostilities were in progress, all these had strenuously opposed Britain's involvement in wars they believed to be unjust, unnecessary, or not in the true interests of Britain.

They had encountered violent opposition, as at Lloyd George's meeting in Birmingham Town Hall, from which he had been smuggled disguised in a policeman's uniform. But the infamous suggestion had never been made that they were 'traitors' or 'fifth columnists'; nor were they interned. These indignities were reserved for Mosley and his friends. Mosley's instructions to British Union read: "To our members my message is plain and clear. Our country is involved in war. Therefore I ask you to do nothing to injure our country, or to help any other power. Our members should do what the law requires of them, and if they are members of any of the forces or services of the Crown, they should obey their orders, and, in particular, obey the rules of their service . . . We have said a hundred times that if the life of Britain were threatened we would fight for Britain again."

I spent a wretchedly sad fortnight with my relatives before returning to Harrow in mid-September. We settled down to the new term in the unreal atmosphere of the 'phoney war' period. There was little or no fighting, but I was shocked when news broke of the first casualties, among whom were two Blackshirt pilots, shot down on a bombing raid over Sylt. I think I had naively believed that sanity would prevail at the eleventh hour, and that peace would be restored before a single life was lost on either side.

Doris and I continued to meet, and to attend the few theatres that still remained open. I would go back to her home for supper, which worried her parents because of my late-night journey back to Harrow, through the total blackout which had been imposed on the outbreak of war, and under the threat of bombs. I would linger at their house in Islington until the last possible moment for catching the last train from the Angel station. If I missed it there was still a chance of catching the last one from King's Cross, and then from Baker Street to Neasden, from where I could walk the rest of the way. To be sure of catching these trains I had to do a good deal of running down Pentonville Road. I learned to feel for every kerb and uneven paving-stone, and I could leap from one to the other in the all-enveloping darkness.

In the summer of 1938, Father Warburton's daughter Grace had married a Frenchman and had gone to live in France. After the wedding we all returned to the school for a short reception before the happy couple left for their honeymoon. Their departure produced one of those trivial incidents that sometimes remain in the memory after more serious matters have faded. Grace's father was obsessed with tidiness: for example, he could never walk from the dining-room door to the table without making a detour to adjust the curtains at the window, or some stray cushion on the settee. On this occasion he stood at the gate, waving a tearful farewell, but before the car taking his beloved daughter away from him had turned the corner and disappeared from sight, he had dashed into the house and back again, dust-pan and brush in hand, to sweep up the confetti littering the garden path.

On one occasion, wanting to please him through this sense of order, I had arranged the spare chairs in the dining-room in perfect formation. There they stood, like Guardsmen on parade, dressed from the right, all present and correct, and ready for inspection. However, my kind thought and actions were not appreciated, but served only to confirm his conviction that I gloried in 'Fascist regimentation', and would one day become a guard in a concentration camp, to which he expected to be consigned. I was never sure whether he really believed such nonsense, or liked to adopt the pose of a potential martyr.

At the King's School there were fewer rules imposed on the staff than there had been at Lewes Grammar School, but Father Warburton disliked our sitting up late at night, consuming his electricity. In the early hours of one morning he surprised us as we were enjoying an informal staff party. He passed some remark, and I made some polite reply, without appreciating what either of us had said. The following morning his wife told us that he had stormed upstairs, thrown open her bedroom door, and exclaimed: "I went to tell the staff to get to bed, and asked them if they realised that it was 3 a.m. That damned fool Hamm asked me: 'Is it really?'" I hold strong views against teachers who intrude their political opinions into the classroom, and I tried to be scrupulously careful to avoid doing this. One day, I had been reading poetry with a class and commenting on poets who were pacifists. I was able to answer, without comment, the polite inquiry from a boy: "Is the Lord Mosley a pacifist, sir?" Many years later I received a letter from one of my ex-pupils of the King's School, now a doctor in Canada, in which he paid me the compliment of saying I was the only teacher who encouraged the boys to "think for themselves."

Soon after Grace Warburton's wedding her young half-sister Jean went to France to spend a long holiday with her, and she was still there when war broke out. Her father was tortured with fears that Jean, who was only fifteen, would be robbed and raped in a France at war. These fears were not altogether unnatural, but to some extent he was a victim of his own wartime propaganda, as well as of his own prejudices. At any rate, he decided that Jean must return home at once, but not unaccompanied. Who could go to France and escort her back to the sanctuary of Harrow? The senior French master seemed the obvious choice, but the Head had a low opinion of his intelligence, and a higher one of mine, in spite of his words about that "damned fool Hamm." So he asked me if I would go, and I readily agreed.

As soon as war had broken out the French had introduced a visa system, so I had to go to the French consulate in London to obtain mine. Here I was introduced to French bureaucracy, with the visa clerk solemnly collecting from me one penny before handing over an application form. I duly completed it, and was granted a visa which allowed me to stay in France for seventy-two hours only. However, I assured the anxious father that I would overstay my permit if necessary in order to rescue his daughter. Under no circumstances would I return without her. In my passport a consular official had entered the purpose of my visit as: "Aller chercher une jeune Anglaise et la ramener en Angleterre", which made me sound like a white-slave trader in reverse of the usual British concept of that role. In Paris I found Jean at the address I had been given, and I confidently expected to be back in London with her well within the permitted seventy-two hours on French soil. But I had reckoned without the bureaucratic mind. I was told that to leave France I would need an exit permit, and that it would take several weeks to obtain this.

Applications for exit permits had to be made in person at the offices of the Paris Surete, later to be made familiar to British television viewers through the Maigret programmes. I joined a long queue, and found ahead of me people with urgent pleas to be allowed to leave France at once. Some of these pleas, as for the welfare of a sick child, were backed by a letter from the British Ambassador in person, but all were being airily waved aside, the tearful applicants being told to come back the next day, or the following week. A cynic was walking up and down the queue, pretending to offer his British passport for sale, price twopence, as it did not appear to carry much weight. On reaching the head of the queue I was told to return the following morning. The rest of the day I spent exploring Paris, particularly its back streets. In any city these are more revealing of its real character than are the main thoroughfares. I noticed many walls covered with antiwar, and even anti-Semitic slogans. The police were nervously alert to any obvious stranger, and I was frequently stopped and questioned: "Vous avez vos papiers, monsieur? I was able to produce my passport and visa, and was allowed to proceed. The next day Gallic logic prevailed, or yielded to my appeal, the exit permit was granted, and I left France with my charge. This was the first of many visits to that delightful land.

One evening a casual conversation in the staff room changed the whole course of my life, at least for the next few years. A colleague was looking down the advertisement columns of the Teachers' World, and readout: " Travelling teacher wanted for the Falkland Islands. Must be able to ride a horse." Remembering my tales of life in Monmouth, he called out to me: "You can ride a horse." Others joined in the banter, and egged me on to apply for the post. Eventually, to halt their teasing, I said that I would write to the Crown Agents for the Colonies for an application form.

Chapter Seven

Geography was not our strong subject, and we vaguely believed that the Falkland Islands were part of the Orkney or Shetland group. The fact that application had to be made to the Crown Agents for the Colonies should have told us otherwise, but we did not give the matter serious thought, as the whole thing was intended as a joke. The application form duly arrived, and I completed and returned it, still with no serious purpose, but just to keep the joke alive. I even went along with it when I was invited to an interview at the Crown Agents' office on Millbank. There I felt sure the joke would end, for I discovered five other applicants, all with better academic qualifications than mine.

When the first applicant emerged from the interview room, the rest of us pounced on him. What questions had he been asked by the board? One was: "Why do you want to go to the Falkland Islands?", and the candidate tried to convince us that he had replied: "Ever since I was a small boy I have wanted to go to the Falklands." When my turn came, my reply to this question was to the effect that I felt I had got into a rut in my present job. This provoked from the chairman of the board the kindly comment: "Not too deep a rut at twenty-four, I trust." When all six applicants had been interviewed I was recalled, and to my astonishment I was offered the post, and was asked how soon I could sail. By this time I had studied the map, and had discovered the Falkland Islands to be small blotches, in the red of the old British Empire, off the coast of Argentina, very far removed from the North of Scotland. Should I go there? Should I leave England in wartime and risk an accusation of cowardice? Should I desert my comrades in British Union, in their campaign to end the war? My personal answer to all such questions lay in my conviction that the war could not possibly last long, and that here was a wonderful opportunity to see the world and advance my career. I was to be offered a three-year 'temporary' engagement in the Colonial Service, but a further and permanent appointment would probably follow. A new vista had opened up before me: an image of myself in later years, reclining in a hammock in some tropical outpost of Empire, bearing the white man's burden, while a dusky maiden fanned me and held a cooling drink to my parched lips. I provisionally accepted the post, and was sent for a medical examination in Wimpole Street, from which I emerged with a clean bill of health, sound in wind and limb.

On the question of deserting my comrades in British Union I decided to consult its Director-General, Neil Francis-Hawkins, and in an interview in his office in Sanctuary Buildings, Great Smith Street, he advised me to accept the post. I was overawed at the thought of meeting such a high-ranking official of British Union, second only to Mosley, the Leader, because I was a very obscure, rank-and-file member of the movement. Its leading figures were Olympian gods to me, to be glimpsed on a distant platform at a monster meeting, or at the head of the column on a march. In later years I got to know some of them personally, and I will give my impressions of them in a later chapter. From my pre-war memories I can give only fleeting pen-pictures.

Raven Thomson, the ex-communist intellectual, became a striking street-corner orator in British Union and a dear friend in later years. There was 'Mick' Clarke, of Bethnal Green, persuaded to mount the platform most reluctantly, when a speaker from N.H.Q. failed to turn up. Mick haltingly read out a policy leaflet, and that was his maiden speech before he thankfully got off the platform to make way for someone else. He too developed into a first-rate speaker, and became a hero-figure in East London. Charming Ann Brock-Griggs, leader of the Women's Section, and a brilliant speaker. These and many others were my heroes and heroines.

Between the outbreak of war and my departure for the Falkland Islands I had been in correspondence with James 'Jimmy' Maxton, the fiery Clydeside I.L.P. member of Parliament. I was thrilled to receive a letter from him inviting me to have tea with him in the House of Commons. He was opposed to the war on pacifist grounds rather than political, but we soon established a tremendous rapport, and discovered we had much in common. I again debunk the nonsense that I supported a 'right-wing' movement. No-one born and bred in the Welsh valleys is likely to go through life touching his forelock to the squire, or supporting 'monetarist' theories.

I was instantly at ease with this great socialist, and did not quail before the piercing gaze from those deep-set, hypnotic eyes. Or rather eye, for one was invariably obscured by the famous lock of unruly hair which flopped over the other, to the delight of every cartoonist, I shamelessly borrowed from him a striking phrase which he had used to describe the unemployed of the thirties, and I used it in many platform speeches, without acknowledgement or apology: "the legions of the lost, and the cohorts of the damned." I have quoted it in my opening chapter.

In those years I was rather exceptionally thin, and Father Warburton would sometimes look across the table at me and quote from Shakespeare's Julius Caesar: "Yon Cassius hath a lean and hungry look." He saw in me, or so he pretended, a political conspirator, and he used to prophesy: "Mark my words, he won't be in the Falklands six months before we read in the newspapers 'Conspiracy in the Falkland Islands'"

A little later he may have thought this forecast had been fulfilled, if not quite in the way he had expected. I stayed with him and his family over Christmas 1939, and during the first week of 1940 with my friends in Islington. On 7 January Doris and I became engaged. The next morning I left the house early, to catch a train to Tilbury, where I boarded the Royal Mail liner Highland Monarch. We sailed at noon, but that night we were halted in the Thames estuary when a ship ahead of ours struck a German mine. We saw the flash and heard the explosion. The ship slowly began to sink, and we dropped anchor. Next morning we moved out into the North Sea, round into the Channel, down the south coast, with our last glimpse of England, and out into the Atlantic.

We crossed the Bay of Biscay, which lived up to its reputation, and then passed into calm, blue seas, with blue skies overhead, heading for our first port of call, Las Palmas, in the Canary Islands. There we were allowed ashore, and I went up into the town to air my elementary Spanish in a bar, for on my appointment to the former Spanish colony of the Falkland Islands I had started learning that language. Did I mishear the time of sailing, or was it brought forward? I returned to the quayside to see the ship, with all my worldly possessions on board, moving away towards the harbour entrance. I ran up and down the quayside until I found a boatman prepared to take me in pursuit. We caught up with the ship just as it was passing out of the harbour and beginning to roll in the open sea. A rope ladder was lowered, and I climbed up the ship's side, and over the rail lined with laughing and cheering passengers. I was on my way.

Chapter Eight

"This windswept, treeless waste", said the Encyclopaedia Britannica of the Falkland Islands. With this sentence I began an article, 'Falkland Impressions', in the November 1954 issue of *The European*. My 'impressions' have not changed with the passage of time, except that some memories may have faded, so I shall borrow extensively from that article in the present chapter.

From the Encyclopaedia, which I had consulted before leaving England, I learned that the islands 'lie some three hundred and fifty miles north-east of Cape Horn. They consist of two main islands — East Falkland and West Falkland, each about fifty miles from north to south and from east to west — and a dozen or so smaller islands, some inhabited by several families and others by a single family or person. If uninhabited islets, some mere rocks, are included, the total runs into more than one hundred . . . The total population is about 2,000, of whom 1,300 live in Port Stanley, on East Falkland.'

There is now communication by air between the Falklands and the mainland, but in those days contact was made only by the Lafonia, a steamer of some six hundred tons, which plied monthly between the Islands, the Chilean port of Punta Arenas, and Montevideo in Uruguay. It never called at an Argentinean port because of the dispute between Britain and Argentina over possession of the islands, with Argentina refusing to recognise the Falkland registration of the little steamer. The thousand-mile voyage between Montevideo and Port Stanley was a nightmare of seasickness, but on the fourth morning we all crawled from our bunks for a first glimpse of the Falklands on the horizon. The smudge began to take shape and form, and became a bare, bleak coastline, behind which towered a broken mountain range, equally uninviting. Then a series of tacks to port and starboard, and the ship entered the seven-mile-long natural harbour, near whose head lies Port Stanley.

Because of the war the Highland Monarch had avoided the South American coast, so that I was deprived of the pleasure of a visit to Rio de Janeiro and other famous beauty-spots. Instead, we had a fortnight with no sign of land, as we lazily steamed across the South Atlantic, constantly tacking and changing direction so as to throw off the marauding German U-boats. Any other ship which appeared on the horizon was anxiously scanned through binoculars, as German surface-raiders were often camouflaged as harmless merchantmen, flying a false flag, and sporting funnels which varied in number and colour almost from hour to hour, so as to negate any descriptions of the ships which might have been radioed to the British navy. It was a fascinating game of hide and seek, but the consequences of detection were rather more serious than in that children's game.

After two weeks, one night we sighted the lights of Montevideo, and the following morning we entered the mouth of the River Plate, where I saw from our deck the wreck of the German battleship Graf Spee. In December 1939 there had been a fierce battle between the Graf Spee and the British cruisers Ajax, Achilles, and Exeter. The Graf Spee had been forced into Montevideo, where her captain sought refuge until she was fit to put to sea and to fight again. There had been a furious battle between the Uruguayan Foreign Office and the British and German embassies in Montevideo. The British government argued that the Graf Spec should be ordered to leave as soon as she was sea-worthy, while the Germans argued that she should not have to leave until she was 'fight-worthy', as she would be a sitting target if she sailed with her guns still out of action. The British government carried the day, and the Uruguayan authorities ordered the Graf Spec to sail.

Under protest, the German captain had put most of his crew on shore, where they had fraternised with British sailors at a dance just a few hours after the battle, and then sailed with skeleton crew to the mouth of the river. There he gave the order to scuttle the ship, and shot himself. As we sailed towards the harbour of Montevideo we passed the gaunt hulk rising out of the water, beneath which it later disappeared, a monument to the futility and tragedy of war.

By English standards Port Stanley is a village, but technically it is a city. In its Anglican cathedral is the throne of the Bishop of the Falkland Islands. His see covered Argentina and Chile, and he visited the Falklands only once every few years. It was on such a visitation that we met and he made the comment on my origins recorded at the beginning of Chapter Two. There is also a small Catholic church in Port Stanley, and a Free Church chapel of some kind.

Life in Port Stanley is not typical of life in the Falklands; to find the true islanders one must go out into 'the camp'. The last Spanish settlers were evicted by the British in 1832, but the countryside is still 'the camp' — el campo. The true Falkland Islander is born in the camp, works all his life in the camp, with only rare visits to Port Stanley, and more often than not dies in the camp. After a few days' teaching in the Port Stanley school I set out for the camp, as a travelling teacher. This meant riding on horses broken in the Spanish style, sitting back on a sheepskin thrown over a high-pommelled saddle, wading or swimming the horses across the Arroyo Malo, the Wicked Brook, or any other stream that might have suddenly become a raging torrent.

I was expected to stay for a week at each settlement or isolated house where there was only one child; and for a fortnight if there were more. At the end of my stay I left an ample supply of homework, and was provided with a new horse and a guide to my next stop. A child might thus receive only two weeks' education in a six-month period.

I settled down to the slow routine of Falkland life, with its menu of mutton, provided in every conceivable form at four meals a day, seven days a week, and its evenings enlivened only with conversation restricted to sheep and the weather, varied with much card-playing and drinking of gin and whisky. When the weather permitted I walked among the seals, sea-lions, spotted sea-leopards, and huge sea-elephants; and I watched the penguins carrying out their intricate manoeuvres with military precision. So would my life have continued, for three years, if fate had not intervened.

We used to listen to the overseas radio programmes of the BBC, and on 23 May 1940 I heard of the arrest and detention, under Defence Regulation 18B, of Mosley and some of his leading lieutenants. My first reaction was to expect my own arrest, but as the days passed I began to think it unlikely that any attention would be paid to a rank-and-file member of British Union now going about his routine duties in a tiny island eight thousand miles from the European centre of war. So I continued with my work until 3 June. On that day my breakfast in an isolated cottage some fifty miles from the little town of Port Stanley was interrupted by the arrival of three members of the Falkland Islands Defence Force, a sort of local Home Guard.

I had seen them riding round a bay and towards the house, but I had continued tranquilly with my breakfast, as it was a Falkland custom for travellers to stop for food and drink at any convenient house on their journey. In fact, if a householder went out for the day he left his door unlocked, so that a traveller could enter and help himself to food, drink and shelter, since exposure to the elements for long periods without warm food could prove dangerous.

The men stopped at the house and entered, and I found three huge fellows towering over me. What were they saying? I was too astonished to believe my ears, but there was no doubt that I had heard correctly: "We have a warrant for your arrest?" (This was well within the six months of Father Warburton's prophesy).

"On what charge?", I asked. "No charge", was the reply, "under the Defence Regulations".

Perhaps it was a tribute to the efficiency of allied propaganda concerning the dangers of the alleged 'fifth column', whose members should be approached with caution, that they were armed with revolvers, and had brought handcuffs with them. They asked me if I would "come quietly", which I found mildly amusing, even under these circumstances. They soon decided that handcuffs were unnecessary, and before we reached Port Stanley, after a three hours' ride, we were firm friends.

Over the last mile we had a race; they had better horses than I, and the situation was reduced to farce as the prisoner urged on his horse, in an attempt to catch up with his gaolers.

As the pace grew faster, my horse stumbled in a pothole, and took off like a jumbo-jet. I was thrown from the saddle, and a metal stirrup hit me in the face, breaking my nose. I arrived in Port Stanley with my face smeared with blood, as if to confirm the rumour sweeping the island that I had violently resisted arrest. The local doctor advised me that nasal operations can be dangerous, and to allow my nose to set itself, unless I was concerned about my appearance. I never have been, and have never worried about a crooked nose, beneath the drooping left eyelid.

On arrival in Port Stanley I was first met by the British army officer in command of the local Defence Force, who told me that if I felt aggrieved I could appeal. I told him I felt considerably aggrieved, but that I experienced some difficulty in making an appeal in the absence of any charge against me, or any explanation for my arrest. He replied that as far as he knew members of 'certain organisations' could be detained. I was then taken by boat to the hulk of a ship lying out in the harbour, and dumped in the hold, with two guards stationed in the wheel-house on the deck above.

Chapter Eight

What was Defence Regulation 18B? On 1 September 1939 the British government had published this regulation, under which the Home Secretary was given power to detain anyone whom he had 'reasonable cause to believe' to be of hostile origin or association, or to have been recently concerned in 'acts prejudicial to the public safety or the defence of the realm.' — Quite clearly, Mosley and his supporters came under neither of these categories, so in May 1940 Regulation 18B was amended, as Defence Regulation 18B (1A). This amendment was framed for the specific purpose of crippling British Union and putting an end to its (perfectly legal) peace campaign. It was retrospective legislation and could thus be applied even to former members of British Union. But first the arrest and internment, without any charge or trial, of Mosley was possible, and took place on 23 May 1940.

Lady Mosley had just given birth to her son Max, so the authorities obligingly left her at liberty until 29 June, when she was thrown into Holloway Prison. At first some seventy or eighty of Mosley's senior officials were arrested, and by the end of June some seven hundred members and sympathisers were interned. Special Branch reports on these men and women confirm that their arrest had nothing whatever to do with the security of the State. It was nothing more than the pursuit of a squalid political vendetta. It is significant that even now (in 1983) papers concerning 18B are being withheld from the Public Records Office, and access to them has been denied to Mosley's son Lord Ravensdale, who wished to consult them as part of his research for a book.

What have the authorities, that mysterious Establishment, still to hide? A glimpse of the truth was revealed in the House of Commons as early as 10 December 1940, when a former Labour Cabinet Minister, Richard Stokes, quoted from a conversation between Mosley and the eminent lawyer of the day, Mr. Norman Birkett, K.C. (later Lord Birkett). (An internee had the right of appeal to a tribunal appointed by the Home Secretary, who had ordered his arrest, but the Home Secretary had the right to reject the recommendations of the tribunal, so that he was a virtual dictator). It is ironic that in Brixton Prison with Mosley in 1940 were members of British Union who between them held every First World War decoration except the Victoria Cross, while Home Secretary Herbert Morrison had only distinguished himself in that war by being a conscientious objector! I respect any man who sincerely holds conscientious objections to military service, but I am sceptical of someone who holds such views while a young man of military age, only to serve in the Cabinet in the next war, and use his powers to imprison political opponents with distinguished military records.

What was this conversation between Mosley and Birkett? Mosley had been cross-examined by Birkett, as chairman of his appeal tribunal, for sixteen hours. The transcript of these proceedings lies among the official papers still withheld from the public, but Richard Stokes quoted the conversation as follows:

Sir Oswald Mosley: "There appears to be two grounds for detaining us:-

(1) A suggestion that we are traitors who would take up arms and fight with the Germans if they landed, and

(2) that our propaganda under mines the civilian morale.

Mr. Norman Birkett: "Speaking for myself, you can entirely dismiss the first suggestion.

Sir Oswald Mosley: "Then I can only assume that we have been detained because of our campaign in favour of a negotiated peace."

Mr. Norman Birkett: "Yes, Sir Oswald, that is the case."

In my dismal dungeon in Port Stanley I found I had a companion, and his story gave me an interesting glimpse of 'the other side of the hill'. His name was Andreas Sollner, and he was a German, born in Eger, in Sudetenland. When the first World War ended he was a boy at school, and found his German teachers replaced by non-German-speaking Czechs the day after the incorporation of his home town into the polyglot state of Czechoslovakia. He had run away to sea, and after a series of adventures had been ship-wrecked on the coast of Chile. Here he became frequently involved in political arguments, and when it was suggested to him that his Czech seaman's papers were not compatible with his pro-German sentiments his reply was always the same: "My papers say I am a Czech, but my heart says I am a German." When eventually Sudetenland became German again he brought his papers into line with his heart by taking out a German passport at a South American consulate.

A few years before the second World War Andreas had returned to sea as a cook on the ship which plied between South America and Port Stanley. There his ship docked on 3 September 1939. Andreas was arrested as an enemy alien, and lodged in the local lock-up, with an armed sentry on guard outside his cell. As his goalers had been his drinking companions for several years the situation was not without humour.

In the early weeks of the war the crew of a German ship which had scuttled in the South Atlantic was brought to the Falkland Islands and interned in a hastily improvised camp, to which Andreas was transferred. Then, in December 1939, the British cruiser Exeter had had to withdraw from its encounter with the Graf Spec. Badly damaged, she managed to crawl to the Falklands, where she made harbour four days later. There she landed some forty seriously wounded men, to the consternation of the meagre staff of the tiny hospital of Port Stanley. In a desperate search for additional staff the hospital authorities interviewed Andreas in his prison camp and asked him if he would become the hospital cook. He replied that as a German he could do nothing to injure Germany or assist Britain, but that he considered cooking for wounded seamen to be humanitarian work, so he would accept their proposal. He was at once released from internment, and from then on worked freely in the hospital. He was allowed to come and go as he pleased in Port Stanley, without even having given his parole.

Later, his former prison-camp companions were transferred to South Africa for internment, and Andreas begged to be allowed to accompany them. But he was persuaded to stay in the Falklands and work in the hospital. Later still, the Exeter's wounded were transferred to South Africa for convalescence. Andreas was deeply touched when her captain, accompanied by the Governor of the colony, came to the hospital to thank him for his services to the seamen. They assured him that they would never forget what he had done. He continued to work at the hospital until the day of my arrest, when he was taken away to our prison ship. It was apparently argued that a German could not be left at liberty while a British subject was interned. Gratitude for his services was conveniently put out of mind. At times he was inclined to feel embittered, but he too had seen the other side of the hill, where lay the real England, so different from that of the Establishment, or of wartime propaganda in his native country.

All this I was to learn from Andreas in the months which lay ahead, when we exchanged life stories and exhausted our stock of anecdotes, absent-mindedly repeating them until we knew them by heart and could fill in any detail the other omitted, like children listening to an oft-told bedtime story. We had so little to do except talk. There were no rules. We got up when we liked and went to bed when we liked. We ate whenever we could summon up enough enthusiasm to cook some of our meagre and unappetising rations, which were brought out to us from the shore once a week. We were allowed on deck by day, but frequent rain and high winds soon drove us below again. Once a week we were taken ashore to the public baths, marched there and back between armed guards.

After a week of this existence I was summoned ashore to appear before a tribunal appointed to hear my appeal against internment. The board consisted of the senior military and naval officers stationed in the Falklands, under the chairmanship of the local colonial secretary, from whom I heard for the first time anything in the nature of a charge against me. It appeared that I had been detained as a member of "a certain organisation, the policy of which is in sympathy with a Government with which His Majesty is at war." Useless to affirm that British Union did not fall into that category. "That is for us to decide", was the chairman's reply.

My appearance before this tribunal was as farcical as any, including that of the unfortunate man who lingered in prison for months because he had written in his diary that the Queen should be replaced by an Italian. Loud and long were his protestations before it was accepted that he was a keeper of bees, and had intended replacing one of his native queens with one from an Italian strain. My diary, letters that I had received, and others that I was about to post, had been seized, and were produced in evidence against me. They were, of course, all totally innocent of anything remotely resembling subversion or treachery; but have you ever tried explaining to a stony-faced tribunal the private jokes and innuendoes of a personal letter? Everything I said was scoffingly rejected. But I had the last word: I was asked if I had anything further to say, and when I thanked them for giving me such a fair and courteous hearing I had the satisfaction of seeing them turn several shades of purple.

A few weeks later I received a letter informing me that the Governor had ordered that my detention should continue, and adding, somewhat superfluously, that my engagement with the government was terminated. Throughout the darkest hours of this tragic farce my sense of humour didn't desert me, and in the post-war years it has blossomed into full bloom as one security scandal after another has been exposed, up to and including the Blunt affair in 1980. Apparently, while patriots were being interned as security risks the security services themselves were being conducted by treacherous Englishmen serving as Russian agents.

Am I prejudiced in arguing that communists in the thirties were security risks, while fascists were not? I will try to examine this question objectively. Many communists were sincere in believing, however mistakenly, that Russia was the workers' paradise, so naturally they would be extremely reluctant to fight against Russia or do anything against her interests. Again, communism denounced patriotism and nationalism as bourgeois concepts, while it exalted internationalism. Communists therefore were easily induced to serve the interests of the Soviet Union in any way possible, not stopping short of espionage and sabotage. Russian plans were further facilitated by the blind hatred of fascism which warped the judgement of our Foreign Office, particularly under Anthony Eden, the wet hen.

Oxford or Cambridge graduates or central European refugees had only to declare themselves 'anti-Fascist' to be admitted to that vital government department, and to our State secrets, with no questions asked. They were recruited by Russian agents, and protected by Russian agents if honest members of the security services became suspicious of their activities and demanded a searching inquiry.

Fascism, on the contrary, was based on an intense nationalism which is now out-moded, but the fact that it was so based meant that it would take its own specific form in each country. There was no equivalent to the Marxist concept of a rigid, universal doctrine, to which every branch of the Communist Party throughout the world was obliged to conform. The nationalism and patriotism on which British Union was based would have made us reject with indignation any proposal that we should assist any foreign power against our own country. It is time that the humbug and hypocrisy of suggestions to the contrary were finally exposed.

From my floating prison I bombarded the Governor of the Falklands with letters claiming my right, as someone detained in a Crown Colony, to appeal to London: first to the Colonial

Chapter Eight

Secretary, then to the Privy Council, and finally to the Crown in person. These letters, and others protesting against the conditions under which I was detained, produced only evasive replies. My friend Andreas exercised his right as an enemy alien to appeal to the International Red Cross, but he met with no greater success as that organisation's local representative was the Governor's daughter.

In reply to a request for fresh vegetable I received from the Governor a haughty reminder that we were at war; he added that he himself had received "no green vegetables for months." I replied that I had not specified the colour of the vegetables I had requested, and added that I was sorry to hear that he had been so sadly deprived. Perhaps he would care to accept some of our dried peas and beans, our staple diet, of which we had more than sufficient? I swept up some of these from the hold, where they had been spilled by rats gnawing at the bags, and packed them into a cardboard box, with much accompanying dirt. The box and letter were taken ashore by the unsuspecting guards. I received no reply to that epistle. After four months in these conditions we were transferred to a cottage on shore in Port Stanley, and there we remained, under house arrest. By way of daily exercise we were allowed out for walks, with our guards following close on our heels. Naturally, we talked to them a great deal about the war. Was it just? Could it have been avoided? Should there not be negotiations for a just and honourable peace?

One day we noticed that our guards were no longer treading on our coat-tails, but were lagging far behind. Under close questioning they shamefacedly admitted that they had been ordered to keep well behind us and not to engage in conversation with us anymore. They had also been instructed to keep us on the move throughout our daily walks. This was too much for our sense of humour. We insisted one day that we were too tired to walk any further, and sat down. When we were ordered to get up we refused, with the plea that our poor feet were killing us.

The guards produced their revolvers, and threatened to shoot us if we did not get up at once. A dangerous game of bluff and counter-bluff ensued. We gambled on their being too nervous to shoot us, as their trembling hands and shaking revolvers confirmed. If they had not been bluffing, or if a revolver had gone off accidentally, I should not have lived to tell this story.

After a few weeks ashore we were unexpectedly informed that we were 'going away', but we were not told our destination, and when it was time to sail we still did not know. On embarking, I handed my final letter of protest to the commanding officer, who politely inquired whether it was 'the soldier's farewell.' We sailed out of Port Stanley harbour, and gradually the Falklands grew fainter on the horizon. It was then that we discovered we were bound for South Africa, but we had no idea whether that was to be our final destination, or only a port of call en route for England.

We made a detour through seas strewn with icebergs, and watched a mountain of flesh, a whale, rise above the water and send its spout gushing towards the heavens. We visited South Georgia, with its two whaling stations, one Norwegian and the other largely Scottish, although the Scots were sometimes supplemented by recruits from the Falklands. These Islanders would leave their sheep for six months in order to try their luck at whaling, and possibly earn a small fortune. After six months of back-breaking work under the harshest of conditions they would return to the Falklands, with money to burn in the quayside pubs before they crawled to their homes in the neighbouring streets, often days after landing. It was midsummer as we lay in the harbour of South Georgia, and the bright sun shone down on the snow and ice which covered the shore, right down to the water's edge, obscuring the grave of the explorer Shackleton. Through the air came the sad lament of the Scottish whalers, far from their native Leith:

"Och, dear me, what shall I dee, If I find oot down here I cann'a mak' it?" Then off we sailed again, north and east, into warmer seas beneath bluer skies, until we entered the great South African naval base of Simonstown. A young shark swam lazily round our ship, and then we berthed. I had set foot in Africa, and had begun a new chapter in my life.

Chapter Nine

Do the much-travelled become blasé about seeing for the first time the few remaining wonders of the world they have not previously encountered? Even today I have seen little of the world, but I had seen much less in 1940, so I was thrilled as I looked for the first time at the majestic heights of Table Mountain, with that extraordinary flat plateau at its top. I saw it for the first time as our ship approached South Africa from the south, and for the second time when I left for home seven months later. Shall I ever return to Africa, in accordance with the old tradition that everyone who enters that mysterious continent falls under its spell and is compelled, drawn by some all-powerful force, to go back at least a second time?

Andreas and I disembarked at Simonstown and were taken to a detention centre at Weinberg, on the coast between the naval base and Cape Town. We were in the custody of Afrikaner military police who scarcely concealed their real attitude to the war under a thin veneer of pretended enthusiasm for the Smuts government. There had been tremendous opposition to South Africa's declaration of war, which had been delayed for several days after the outbreak of war in Europe. The Defence Minister, Oswald Pirow, whom I was to meet later in England, had resigned in protest. A Bill to introduce conscription had been defeated, and volunteers could choose to serve only in South Africa, if they so wished. Smuts, while paying lip-service to freedom and democracy, used internment ruthlessly against his political opponents, among whom was the future Prime Minister and later President of the Republic, John Vorster. From our Afrikaner custodians we received wonderfully kind treatment, as if we were honoured guests rather than internees.

After a few days Andreas and I were moved to separate internment camps, and I never saw him again. On a Thursday evening I left Cape Town by train on the one-thousand-mile journey to Johannesburg, where I arrived on the Saturday morning. The tedium of this journey was relieved and enlivened by the friendliness of my Afrikaner escorts, and by the contrasting views from the train's wide bay-windows. At first we passed through the narrow coastal belt of almost tropical vegetation; but then came the arid wastes of the Great Karoo desert, before we entered the flat veldt of the Transvaal.

At the stations where we stopped I was able to observe apartheid in operation, with separate waiting-rooms, toilet facilities, and benches for whites, blacks, and coloureds. But surely apartheid did not operate under the benevolent Jan Christian Smuts? Was it not the brain-child of the wicked nationalists, who did not come to power until 1948? This myth has been created and nourished in many a British school and university, where serious research is not encouraged lest it reveal that the word apartheid was first publicly used by Smuts himself. I also saw the Smuts version of the system in the shape of shanty towns of tents, and hovels constructed from old petrol tins. Most of these have long since been cleared by successive nationalist governments.

Our train pulled into the hustle and bustle of Johannesburg's main station, and I was taken by car to Leeuwkop (Lion's Head) internment camp, on the open veldt some ten miles from the city. After 'reception' (a formal taking of particulars, and a cursory search which spared one the indignities of the British prison system) the inner gates of the camp were opened, and I was handed over to an internee, who took me to the hut to which I had been assigned.

A new arrival from the outside world was always a source of great excitement, and I was greeted by a babel of German voices asking who I was and where I came from. My reply (in German) that I was British was received with astonishment, and my explanation that I was interned because of my membership of a fascist organisation evoked more than surprise. Most of the inmates of the hut turned out to be communists, or other refugees interned for entering South Africa illegally. I was escorted back to reception and handed over to an internee from 'the other side', an area of huts well apart from those of the communists, and accommodating people who favoured another ideology, or none.

My new companions were not all Germans, but included representatives from almost every country in Europe. They had been interned for a wide variety of reasons, the anonymous letter or secret report of the agent provocateur being high on the list. My personal position was delicate: I was opposed to the war, but did not wish to see my country defeated by any foreign power. This view was respected by the Germans, who used good-humouredly to refer to me as 'the British consul'. We lived together in good comradeship, but our discussions on the war, and the possible fate of our respective countries, were regulated by a mutually-imposed formality.

The camp commandant interfered little with its internal administration, which was carried out by the internees, under the leadership of an elected lagerfuhrer. We prepared and cooked our own meals, and kept our quarters clean by rota, each man doing his allotted share of stubedienst and lager-dienst. Communication with the outside world was officially restricted to censored mail and occasional visits, of which I naturally received none. But the camp had been a Bantu prison, and some of the 'boys' came into the camp from the prison to which they had been transferred, and worked there by day. With their co-operation, and the exercise of considerable ingenuity, a daily newspaper was smuggled into the camp. (The German word for newspaper might be known to the camp guards, so zeitung became schwalbe — a swallow — in our private argot). A cunningly concealed radio not only received news and messages, but transmitted camp information to interested parties outside. The neglected art of conversation was revived in the camp, and our favourite occupation was to promenade in twos and threes in the cool of the evening, putting the world to rights in long discussions prefaced with the pathetic words nach dem Krieg — "after the war".

As Christmas 1940 approached a little extra fare was collected, saved up from Red Cross parcels, or salvaged from our meagre rations, and when the time came a brave attempt was made to celebrate in the traditional way. On Christmas Eve a German priest-internee sang Midnight Mass, in a hut crammed with every man in our section of the camp, Catholic and non-Catholic alike. Just after midnight he addressed us briefly, his voice ringing out: Heute ist Weihachten, und heute gibt's nur einen Wunsch in jedem Herz . . . die Friede. What a longing for peace welled up in every heart, German. French, British, all Europeans.

This German priest had been interned on some trumped-up allegation that he was plotting to blow up a bridge! He accepted his fate with stoic philosophy, and spent much of his time in a small cell which had been allotted to him so that he could say his daily office and offer Mass at a small altar. A few of us were very fond of him, and we used to invite him to join us for coffee. We would go to his cell in a small procession, bow to him in mock solemnity, and intone: Hen Vater, Du bist eingeladen, mil den lieben Kameraden eine Tasse Kaffee zu trinken. He would accept our invitation with the same mock gravity.

Among the internees we saw the tragic effects of depression, and on one occasion were just in time to take a rope away from an old man who was about to hang himself in a mood of black despair. But I had been drawn into a small group with firm ideas on maintaining our morale. My closest friend was Heinz, who had been selected to represent Germany in the Berlin Olympic Games of 1936. In training he had fallen and broken both his legs, so he had to be excluded. The legs set crookedly, but otherwise he was a magnificent physical specimen. He was also of a serious turn of mind, and had been appointed camp librarian.

The library was in a small hut to which he held the key. He

laid down and enforced his own rules, so that the hut was open during restricted hours only. At all other times he and I locked ourselves inside, and read and studied in silence. During my six months in the camp I used practically no English. I spoke German or French, together with the few words of Afrikaans I had picked up. Much of the time I spent in translating from French to German, from Spanish to Italian, and so on, without using English as an intermediary language.

If Christmas Day, 1940, had been a rather solemn occasion, the New Year of 1941 was ushered in very differently. No alcoholic drink was allowed in the camp, but in the camp shop fruit was cheap and plentiful. Over the preceding weeks we had been buying apples, oranges, peaches, bananas, pineapples — in short, every conceivable fruit — and had been chopping them up and leaving them to ferment in a tub. On New Year's Eve we started to drink this noxious brew, and it soon began to have its effect. I have vague memories of the whole camp walking round and round in procession under the hot and cold showers. My last memory is of being tossed high in a blanket. I do not remember falling asleep, but I awoke to find myself tied hand and foot with rope, with most of my hair cut off, and my body smeared all over with black boot-polish. I was not feeling my best at roll-call on that first morning of 1941.

We were always on guard against the 'nark' to be found in most camps and prisons, and would not confide any secrets to anyone outside a closed circle of intimate friends. One day two Germans beckoned me aside, out of ear-shot of the others, and told me they wished to ask me a question. But before doing so they asked me to answer with a straight yes or no, and if the answer were no to promise them that I would forget what they had asked. I gave the promise, and they asked me if I would join them in a plan to escape. I answered: "Yes."

For the Germans in the camp, escape was the prelude to a trek of several hundred miles to Lourenco Marques, in what was then Portuguese East Africa. There the German consulate would take the escaped man under his wing, and a passage would be arranged for him on a neutral but friendly ship.

Many escapees reached Germany by devious routes, after thrilling adventures. The first step, of course, was to get out of the camp. By day armed guards surrounded the compound, and also the large garden at its rear, where we were allowed to work, growing a few vegetables. At the end of the afternoon a bell would summon us into an inner compound, where the roll was called. When the commandant was satisfied that all were present the guards were withdrawn from around the garden, and took up positions around the inner perimeter until morning.

A would-be escaper had therefore to hide in the garden until after roll-call — from which his absence had to be concealed. Then, when the guards had been withdrawn, he had only to slip through the barbed wire to freedom. At the signal for roll-call the occupants of the first hut would line up to be counted, after which they would fall out. One of their number would then rapidly crawl through holes in the walls of the huts. Suitably disguised by a quick change of clothing, he would emerge further along the line, and fall in with the others, to be counted once again, replacing the missing man, who was hiding in a hole in the garden. By this method an escape often went unnoticed for weeks, until a change of method in calling the roll rendered this particular plan no longer feasible.

Escape by night from the inner compound was more difficult, but in the early months of 1941 I joined a small, carefully selected group in an attempt to dig a tunnel from the camp centre, underneath the barbed wire, to the outside world. We began digging under the floor of a store-room, carefully replacing the boards early each morning before creeping back to our beds, which we had left when everyone else was asleep. Our main problem was the disposal of the excavated earth, but we made steady progress, lighting our tunnel with stolen electric light bulbs as we advanced. I had no idea where I would go if I escaped, but I did not have to answer the question.

The South African authorities had agreed to forward to London my petition for release, which the Governor of the Falkland Islands had returned to me. Eventually it reached the desk of the then Colonial Secretary, Lord Moyne, by a coincidence father of Lady Mosley's first husband. He cabled the South African government requesting my release, and I was called to the commandant's office in April 1941, to be told that I would be going home within a few days, as soon as the formalities had been completed. I was further told that I would be released 'on certain conditions'. Immediately I protested that I was not prepared to accept any conditions, since to do so would imply admission of some guilt. A few days later I was recalled to the office and told that the only conditions would be local ones: that I should not break my journey between Johannesburg and Cape Town, and that I should leave South Africa on the first available ship. I agreed, and packed my few possessions, ready to be taken to Johannesburg that evening to catch the night train.

During my life I have received many more brickbats than bouquets, and I have never been influenced by either; neither abuse nor flattery affects me. But even the most cynical can sometimes be moved by some spontaneous gesture of kindness, and I experienced such a gesture that evening. As I stood in the courtyard between the camp's inner and outer gates, waiting for my transport, my comrades flocked to the inner gate and stood there to sing the hymn of farewell sung at German military funerals. I could not fail to be touched as they sang, at the height of this tragic war between Britain and Germany: Ich hat' ein Kameraden, ein besseren findst Du nicht. . .

When I was back in England I often thought of my friends in South Africa. What were their feelings as they saw all hopes of a German victory fading away? Were they still more depressed when they realised that there could be no victory for either

England or Germany, but only for Soviet communism? Or, as they looked through the barbed wire and across the South African veldt, did they dream of a new Europe arising, phoenix-like, from the ashes of the old, a continent united at last ?

Chapter Ten

At Cape Town I boarded a ship for England. My exit permit from South Africa gave my occupation as 'internee', but this did not deter the purser from allotting me a first-class cabin. In the excitement of my release I had forgotten to check that all my personal possessions had been returned to me, and I suddenly realised that I had not got my passport. I spoke to the purser about this, and he assured me that all would be well as "someone would be meeting me when we berthed". Suspicions that all was not well arose in my mind, but he reassured me, and I settled down to enjoy life on board.

We sailed northward, up the west coast of Africa, until we lay off Lagos, in the sweltering tropical heat. The paint on the rails blistered, and the metal parts were too hot to touch. I looked down into the water at the locals who had rowed out in primitive craft to beg for pennies, which the passengers threw down to them. Down they dived, as agile as dolphins, emerging with a coin, to shout their thanks and invoke God's blessing on the good lady who had thrown them a penny — and on her husband too.

One morning we were called on deck early to catch our first glimpse of the Rock of Gibraltar, towering out of the sea. We lay in its harbour for some days, and I went ashore several times, exploring the little town, and climbing to the highest point of the Rock for the ritual visit to the apes, and to look across the narrow strait to the coast of North Africa.

Our passenger list was swelled by our taking on board the last of Gibraltar's civilian population, who were being evacuated to England because of the threat of a German invasion through Spain, and to preserve the Rock's meagre food supplies. Among our new passengers I became particularly friendly with a

Chapter Ten

Spanish couple and their daughter Blanca (or Blanquita in the diminutive which is the mark of affection in Spanish). Blanquita remained my good friend through correspondence, and we met again in London later on. At last, late one night, we sailed from Gibraltar. When I awoke the next morning I thought the ship seemed strangely motionless. I went on deck and found that we had turned back during the night, because of U-boats reported lying in wait out in the Atlantic. Our spirits were not raised when we heard our ship named in a taunting broadcast by William Joyce, the Lord Haw-Haw of the German radio English language broadcasts.

At last we put to sea again, and sailed far out into the Atlantic before turning northward, so that we passed to the west and north of Ireland before turning into the Clyde. We inched our way up its lower reaches and then through its industrial areas, until we docked at Glasgow. Wondering what sort of reception awaited me, I braced my shoulders and strode down the gang-plank to step on British soil for the first time in eighteen months.

It was now June 1941. As I was making myself known to an immigration officer as a passenger without a passport I was approached by a civilian who identified himself as a police officer who, 'by virtue of his office', was inviting me to accompany him to Glasgow's police headquarters. I received the impression that this courteous invitation was in fact a firm command, and I went with him in a police car.

In his office he informed me that he had been instructed to serve on me a restriction order, requiring me to inform him of the address to which I proposed to travel, to report to the police any change of address, and to report to them once a week.

In the strongest possible terms I protested that I had been tricked. While in South Africa I had made it clear that I would not accept any restrictions other than the local ones listed in my release papers, and that I would not leave the camp if there were any suggestion of further restrictions. The police officer pretended to sympathise with me, and said that in his opinion the way I was being treated was 'not cricket'; a most unusual remark from an officer in a city not renowned for its prowess at that so-English game. Gradually he talked me into a most reluctant acceptance of the order, whose details were inscribed, in red ink, all over the front and back of the identity card with which I was then issued. These formalities having been completed, I left the police headquarters and booked into a Glasgow hotel, the name of which was noted in police records.

Where should I go next? My parents had shown no sympathy with or understanding of my political beliefs, nor for me during my internment. My one contact was the faithful Doris, who had been evacuated with her Civil Service colleagues from London to Morecambe. So to Morecambe I travelled, and there I managed to get a room in the guesthouse where Doris and her friends were billeted.

What should be my next step? My opposition to the war and the indignities I had suffered through internment, and the unsatisfactory manner of my release, had not shaken my basic principle that I must remain loyal to my country, 'right or wrong'. Britain was in grave danger of invasion, and it was obviously my duty to volunteer for the forces and play what small part I could in my country's defence. So on arrival in Morecambe I registered for service, and was asked which of the three services I had chosen. This was a question I had not considered, so on the spur of the moment I opted for the Royal Air Force, but just why I cannot say.

I had very little money, so a job was vitally important while I was awaiting my medical examination and call-up. I found employment in the NAAFI stores which had opened in the peace-time holiday camp at Heysham Towers, on the outskirts of Morecambe. This work would have entitled me to exemption from military service, but I did not relish the idea of civilian life while most men of my age were in the forces, so I declined the manager's offer to apply for exemption for me.

Life in Morecambe was agreeable. All the girls in the house were pleasant and seemed to take pity on me, moved in part by my tales of internment. One, a talented artist, actually insisted on painting my portrait in oils. I sat for her as patiently as my nature would allow, but I was not suited to the role of male model, and the painting was never finished.

Once a week I had to report to the local police. I tried to win the confidence of the officer to whom I reported, and to persuade him to reveal the dark secrets alleged to be contained in my dossier, compiled during the years when (he assured me) I had been 'under police observation'. It used to lie, tied with red tape, on the desk before him during our conversations. One day, after much protesting that he dared not reveal anything, he opened it apparently at random and read out a statement that at one time I "had been associating with a girl called Edna . . . ", my friend of earlier Pontypool days. The 'association' had consisted of meeting her once or twice for coffee while I was home on holiday from Harrow. The recording of this trivial circumstance gave me an immediate respect for the efficiency of the Special Branch, a respect which has grown rather than diminished over the years. I have never resented their attention, as all my activities have been strictly legal, and I have never had anything to conceal.

At last came an order to report at Kendal for my medical examination. I was passed A1, and I was then interviewed by a RAF officer who expressed the opinion that I was "just the sort of man they were looking for" — for the Service Police! This was not one of the roles I had visualised, but, as always, I was prepared to try anything.

The officer was about to affix his signature to my papers when, most apologetically, he said he had to ask me, as merest formality, whether I had ever been in trouble with the police. I replied that I had no convictions, but had been interned under Defence Regulation 18B. He said he would have to refer the matter to the Air Ministry, and that there would be a delay, possibly of several months. I told him this would not suit me at all, and he made a comment which I thought at the time was most unfair to another service: "Try the Army, my boy. They'll take anybody!"

Later, during a barrack-room brawl, or in a crowded garrison town on pay-night, there were occasions when I thought there might possibly be some grain of truth in his statement. My papers were passed to a Colonel Blimp at the next table, who was delightfully vague about 18B. At first he said: "I see you've been a prisoner of war." I mildly corrected this error, and again explained that I had been interned under Defence Regulation 18B. "Something to do with peace, wasn't it?" he inquired, and I agreed.

Soon I encountered for the first time Army selection methods in operation. Later I was to become more familiar with them: much placing of dots in squares and circles, always with the result that a civilian butcher was posted to the Army Pay Corps, while an accountant became a butcher in the Army Catering Corps. I had never received any technical education, and at school I had broken the heart of my woodwork master by producing, after much discarding of wasted wood, a mortice-joint held in place by hidden glue and shavings. So I was obviously 'just the man they were looking for' in the Royal Armoured Corps. I duly received my call-up papers, ordering me to report to Catterick Camp.

Doris insisted that I must first go home and see my parents, and she came with me to Pontypool. I notified the Morecambe police that I was leaving for Pontypool, and that I would return by a night train and catch an almost immediate connection to Catterick. This would leave me with little or no time to report back to the Morecambe police, which they insisted I must do. My train back was late, and I had no time to report. I heard from Doris later that the police had called at the house that afternoon to find out why I had failed to report, and to check on my whereabouts.

Where was I by that time? I had reported at Catterick Camp, and had handed in my identity card, bearing the written restrictions under which I had been obliged to report to the police. It was taken from me without comment, and in return I was issued with an army uniform, and full kit, including a rifle. By this sudden metamorphosis I was transformed from an alleged danger to the security of the State, a person who must report to the police at least once a week, into 7944045 Trooper Hamm E.J., armed with a rifle with which to defend the rolling plains of Catterick against the enemy. Strange indeed are the workings of the bureaucratic mind. I had left Civy Street behind me, and the Army was about to undertake the Herculean task of attempting to turn me into a soldier.

I have never lost my interest in the Falkland Islands and South Africa, or in anything which reminds me of those eventful years of 1940 and 1941. Early in 1980 I watched a BBC television documentary on the battle of the River Plate and the sinking of the "Graf Spee". Every shot of Montevideo brought back memories of the week I had spent there on my way to the Falklands. In December 1979 many British and German survivors of the battle had travelled to Montevideo from all parts of the world, to commemorate its 40th anniversary, and there they were joined by some of the large German population of Buenos Aires. At the end of the day Britons and Germans laid wreaths on the grave of the captain of the Graf Spee. The wreaths laid, they stepped back, came to attention, and sang that touching farewell to whose strains I had left Leeuwkop Internment Camp in April 1941: Ich hat' ein Kameraden, ein besseren findst Du nicht. . .

It was a traumatic experience for me to watch the television news pictures of the Argentine invasion of the Falkland Islands and of the successful counter-stroke by Britain's Task Force. I knew every inch of the ground between San Carlos and Port Stanley, and every shot brought back memories of my ride across the camp in March 1940, and my return journey, under escort, in June of that year.

Could not this tragedy have been avoided? The Franks Report summarised the abortive negotiations over the years, between Britain and Argentina. Consideration was given to granting sovereignty over the islands to Argentina, who would then lease them back to Britain, but no agreement was reached, and Argentina's patience was exhausted, so that she resorted to force. Successive British governments had rejected the alternative to a settlement — the creation of a 'Fortress Falklands'. Now Mrs. Thatcher informs us that this is the 'only option.'

It was rather late in the day for Britain to express concern over the fate of the islanders, neglected or exploited for years. Why else had the population almost halved since the war? By 1982 the education of Falkland children was no longer utterly dependent upon a lone travelling teacher treking across the camp, for many were now flying to good schools in Argentina. No longer had the seriously ill or injured to be flown 8,000 miles to Britain, because of the inadequate resources of Port Stanley's tiny cottage hospital. Now, by errors on both sides, goodwill between Britain and Argentina has been destroyed, and the placid life of the islanders is gone forever, unless sanity eventually prevails, and some agreement is reached between two old friends.

Chapter Eleven

The Royal Armoured Corps incorporates the original Royal Tank Regiment and elements created by the mechanisation of former infantry and cavalry regiments, especially the latter. Diverse traditions thus combine to form its attitudes towards the rest of the Army, and warfare itself.

The tank had evolved from the concept of transferring the principle of the battleship to land, thus creating a 'land ship' which should combine the heavy defensive armour of its naval counterpart with the mobility of cavalry. Naval influence had suggested 'Dreadnaught' as a suitable motto for the Tank Regiment, but this was modified to 'Fear Naught'. The cavalry influence divided a tank regiment not into companies and platoons, but into squadrons and troops. A company commander was a squadron leader, and the lowest rank, with which I entered and left the Army, was that of a trooper.

Our early days in the Army alternated between hours on the parade ground, being drilled until we at least "looked like soldiers, even if we weren't", and attending lectures. An early lecture was on the history of the tank and of the regiment, and I listened intently for the name of that famous soldier who had done more than any other to develop the tank, and overcome the opposition of the War Office to this invention. His books had been largely ignored by the War Office, but avidly read by the German High Command, who were the first to learn their lessons and put them into practice in their 'blitzkrieg'.

A prophet is not without honour save in his own country, and that was the fate of Major-General J.F.C. Fuller, whose name was never mentioned, because of his being Sir Oswald Mosley's most eminent military supporter in British Union. After his death

I had the honour of representing the Mosleys at a memorial service for him in Westminster Abbey.

I was trained as a wireless operator, and after reaching a certain standard of proficiency I was awarded my 'sparks' badge to wear on my sleeve, under my tank emblem. But each tank crew member was expected to show a reasonable proficiency in the duties of the other members, so I learned to drive everything from a light truck or Bren-gun carrier to a 50-ton tank, and to fire any weapon from a six-pounder to a revolver.

When I joined the Army I wondered what effect my unorthodox entry would have on my military career. Within a few days I was ordered to report to my squadron leader, who told me that the unit security officer had informed him that I had been 'talking foolishly' in the NAAFI canteen. I at once recognised this as bluff. For the first few days of Army life a recruit is so busy cleaning and polishing his equipment, and learning how to lay it out on his bed, with every article correctly positioned in minute detail, that he has no time to poison himself with NAAFI tea. I assured the officer that I did not even know where the canteen was, and called his bluff by asking him if he were aware of the unusual circumstances of my entry into the Army. He admitted that he did, but made it clear that he was not interested in my politics as long as I was genuinely prepared to soldier. "Would this be O.K. by you?" he asked. I assured him that such an arrangement would be "O.K. by me".

Nothing more was said for several months, and my training continued. I turned also to sport, and as there were no facilities for rugby I took up cross-country running. As a result, I left the Army with a record as undistinguished as that of my schooldays, from which I had emerged with one prize only, awarded for my skill in debating. I left the Army with one medal: for running. Ever since, I have avoided formal functions at which "decorations will be worn." I suspect that among the medals and ribbons of the Victoria Cross and other orders my simple medal, with its inscription "7944045 Trooper Hamm, E.J., Catterick Garrison Crosscountry Team" might make an odd impression.

As a runner I was coached by a Sergeant-Major Instructor from the Army School of Physical Training, a fierce little man who struck terror into our hearts on our first encounter. After several weeks on the barrack square we entered the gymnasium for the first time, and he addressed us thus: "You have come here on a six weeks' course. The first three weeks we break you, the second three weeks we make you. I want you to know that when you are in my gymnasium you are just as much on parade as if you were on the barrack square. When I give you an order to move, I don't expect you to walk, I don't expect you to run. I expect you to JUMP!" And we did, a foot into the air.

But between us there soon developed that strange affinity which often binds athlete and coach, and he exercised an enormous influence over me. Before a race he would face me across a table, fix me with his hypnotic eyes, and say: "I want you to run like the hammers of hell!" I never knew what they were. But I did. His methods worked, and I used to win. The prize was usually a box of cigarettes, a jewel beyond price to smokers in those days of rationing, but rather wasted on me as a non-smoker. After a gruelling race I would stagger drunkenly to the door of my barrack-room, clutching my box of cigarettes.

My comrades would be waiting for me, poised to seize the prize and light up. I enjoyed much temporary popularity, which was dimmed only when I announced one day that in view of the atrocious weather I did not intend to run. My protests were howled down, and there was a passionate appeal to my loyalty to my comrades. I was forced out into the rain and high winds, to run, to win, to return with more cigarettes. I was sad to notice that few young men volunteered for any form of sport. This particularly irked our boxing instructor, a former champion of the Metropolitan Police. He would catch the eye of a particular friend of mine and myself, and we would reluctantly step forward and put on the gloves. Then we would go through the motions, circling each other cautiously, giving each other an occasional light tap. "You're not hurting each other!" he would bellow, but we had no intention of spoiling our friendship with too much belligerence, and we would continue our cautious manoeuvres for the rest of the bout.

No further reference was made to my political background, and the time came for my squad to be posted to sundry Royal Tank regiments. The postings went up on the notice-board, every name except mine. I was given no explanation, and asked none. Orders had evidently been received from outside the unit, from some political boffin in the War Office or elsewhere. I received several periods of leave, and on one of these an incident extended still further my stay at Catterick.

Neighbours in Brynwern had a daughter whom I had taught in my student-teaching days who was now a young woman, a few years younger than I. I was a friend of all the family, and I struck up a warm friendship with the girl. (Doris had decided that our politics were not compatible, and had broken off our engagement). We soon exhausted the pleasures provided by Pontypool's cinemas, and one evening we decided to take "a quiet walk in the woods". On our way home we were hurrying down a steep slope when I felt my feet slipping under me. Gallantly, or perhaps ungallantly, I let go her hand and jumped, thinking I was near the bottom of the slope. But I was far from the bottom, and I crashed from a considerable height with some force, taking the brunt of the fall on my right hand. Next morning my wrist was heavily swollen. I reported to an Army Medical Officer in the town, who diagnosed a broken wrist, and gave me a certificate extending my leave. Off I was sent to the Royal Gwent Hospital in Newport, to have the fracture set and my wrist encased in plaster. I now enjoyed a long spell at home, where I was wined and dined by the good people of the town, who imagined a wounded warrior had come home from battle. I could, of course, no longer give the immaculate salute I had learned on the barrack-square at Catterick; instead I caught the eye of every passing officer with a flashing eyes-right or eyes-left.

On my return to Catterick the mysterious back-room boffin's delaying tactics continued, but he must have relented at last. Some eleven months after my entry into the Army I was posted to a service unit. I had found Catterick a cold, bleak place, and I had hoped for a posting to the warmer south, but this was not to be. My destination was Stobbs Camp, near Hawick in Scotland, and I crossed the border for the first time. The camp lay in a hollow, amid the encircling hills, over which the 'Scotch mist' would sweep: a driving rain which reduced visibility to a minimum.

The camp was shared with us by the Black Watch, and at the end of each day we heard them returning to camp long before we saw them. At first it would be a stray note from the pipes, blown on the winter's wind. Then the stirring tune became recognisable, as they marched into camp to the strains of their proud regimental march Cock of the North. They were indeed cocks of the North, proud of their regimental history and of their individual fighting qualities.

I have no record of how long I spent at Stobbs Camp, or at any other, but my stay there was terminated abruptly, as it was elsewhere. The boffin was at work again. I received a sudden posting to another Royal Tank regiment, this time to the south of England. How many times this sort of thing happened, or in what chronological order, I cannot clearly remember. I would be out of camp on a day pass, and would return shortly before midnight, well after lights-out, and with a rigid blackout in force. I would find a note pinned to my blankets, and would read it by torchlight, under the blankets, to learn that I was to leave early the following morning for another regiment, at the other end of the land. A frenzied packing in the dark would follow, and I would set off soon after reveille.

Chapter Eleven

I recall moving, but not necessarily in this order, from Scotland to Hythe on the Kent coast; from Kent back to Scotland, to Ayreshire on the west coast: from there back to Kent, to the Faversham-Ashford-Maidstone area. My boffin eventually ran out of Royal Tank regiments, and was reduced to posting me to the Fife and Forfar Yeomanry. As a Welshman who had lived for years in London I found it somewhat difficult to sing with much enthusiasm the praises of "The wee cooper o' Fife " or "A hundred pipers and a' ".

Was there any justification for my being regarded as a security risk who should be posted at short notice from one unit to another? If I am asked whether I talked politics in the Army, I must reply that I did; openly and frankly, as most other soldiers did in barrack-room arguments, and at ABCA meetings. The Army Bureau of Current Affairs was supposed to be an information service, designed to keep us informed on world affairs, but many of us regarded it as a propaganda exercise, and we freely expressed our criticisms at question time. On one occasion we were lectured on German concentration camps, at a special ABCA meeting for the whole brigade in the presence of the Brigadier himself. At question time I innocently asked whether concentration camp inmates were given any trial, or were sent there without previous judicial process, as were 18B internees. The officer-lecturer exploded: "I don't know anything about 18B. I'm a soldier, not a politician — thank God!" I was posted the following morning.

This treatment was disturbing and irritating. It broke up barrack-room friendships and dislocated my mail. For some time I accepted it philosophically, but eventually I asked for and was granted a private interview with my squadron leader, and later with the colonel of the regiment. They were all sympathetic, and they gave me no reason to doubt their assurance that they had no part in the business, which they found most distasteful. One officer went so far as to advise me to desert! I rejected this advice, and settled down to a strict observance of Army rules and regulations when necessary, combined with an utter disregard for them when they would have interfered with my personal pleasure.

For example, when stationed at Hythe I much enjoyed a weekly ride on a horse from stables in the town. The proprietor was a lady who had much better horses than the hacks often found in riding-schools. She used to buy the rejects of racing-stables, not quite up to racing standards, and she had one particularly fierce mare, a blood-relation of a pre-war Derby winner. Before she allowed me to ride it, she warned me that it had thrown every previous rider, including one who had ridden in the Grand National. On this animal I enjoyed many a wild gallop, and the battle of wills between a horse as determined to throw me as I was to remain in the saddle.

Eventually the mare won, and I had a heavy fall, which injured my back. The M.O. put me on "light duties", which involved working in the cook-house from reveille to lights-out, scrubbing greasy pots and pans. Later, when I was at another camp in Kent, I used to travel to Hythe to ride at every possible weekend, dispensing with the formality of applying for a pass, which might have been refused.

When in Ayrshire I used to be invited to go into Carlisle with the weekly ration truck, which would drop me in the town and pick me up for the return journey. Again I dispensed with a pass, and an evil day arrived when I was stopped by the military police. Being unable to produce a pass I was taken to their barracks, where they confirmed my identity before ordering me to return to camp at once. A new posting followed almost immediately, and I gave the matter no further thought.

On my first morning in the new unit, as I was preparing for the customary formal interview of a new arrival with the squadron leader, I was told that I was on a charge; a somewhat inauspicious start. The military police had sent on a charge against me of being more than five miles from my camp 'without lawful authority.' There ensued one of those comic-opera scenes which enliven the monotony of Army life. This one was the cause of bewilderment to some new recruits who witnessed it.

They were waiting to see the squadron leader when I was marched in for my interview with him, wearing my beret, of course. I asked him for a private interview, and this was granted, but he decided first to hear the charge against me. I came out from the first interview, and prepared to march back in again to face the charge. But this time I was a prisoner, my beret had to be snatched off my head, and I had to be escorted at front and rear.

The raw recruits, fresh from training unit, trembled at the barked: "Cap off! Prisoner and escort, quick march!" They looked as if they thought I must be facing at least a charge of murder. The squadron leader, however, took the view that the charge was a trivial matter and should be dismissed; but all military police charges must be heard by the commanding officer of the regiment, so I was remanded to appear before him. The private interview with the squadron leader was to follow the preliminary hearing, so out I was marched, still capless and under escort. Back on went the beret, and back in I marched, unescorted, for my private interview. Then I marched out again.

By this time the colonel had arrived, to hear any charges referred to him. "Cap off! Prisoner and escort, quick march!" came the order. In I went — and out again — with the charge finally dismissed. The new recruits to the regiment must have formed an extraordinary impression of an Army in which the same soldier kept popping in and out of office doors, sometimes wearing a beret, sometimes capless, sometimes under escort, sometimes alone.

At the height of the war the Army still played soldiers with much enthusiasm. On one occasion it was my unhappy lot to be guarding the tank-park at Catterick on Christmas Day, and my Christmas night was not improved by being detailed for the 2a.m stint. When I was relieved at four the guard commander asked what had been going on outside. I was mystified, and he explained that the orderly officer had called and remarked that there was "a very smart sentry on duty".

What had I done to earn such extravagant praise? I had seen a snow-clad figure approaching through the darkness, and I had challenged him. It had proved to be the orderly officer, who told me he had noticed an abandoned vehicle on the edge of the tank park, and asked me to investigate it with him. Wanting to open the radiator cap to check whether there was water in the tank, he found it frozen in position, so he asked me if he could borrow my rifle and knock the cap off with its butt.

My training reminded me of the answer I should give, without a moment's hesitation: under no circumstances must a sentry hand over his rifle to anyone: not to the highest-ranking officer, not even to the King or Queen. He agreed that I was "quite right", and went into the guard-room to sing my praises.

In one service unit we played games even more enthusiastically than at Catterick. A three-man guard was required for the colonel's office, but each of the four squadrons was required to detail a man. The four men would parade for inspection by the orderly officer, and the smartest man of the four would be ordered to fall out. He would be excused the guard and all other duties for the day, except delivering the occasional message for the colonel. He was 'stick-man', carrying an officer's cane for the day as a symbol of this high office, a symbol regarded as somewhere above a field-marshal's baton (an object which I never found at the bottom of my knapsack).

There was intense rivalry between the four squadrons for this honour, and each would detail its chosen man some weeks before the great day. Every possible minute in the intervening period would be spent on pressing an immaculate crease into trousers, brushing invisible specks of dust from the beret, and polishing everything imaginable. Consequently, four immaculate tailors' dummies paraded for inspection, and the orderly officer would have to exercise the proverbial wisdom of Solomon to decide to whom the 'stick' should be awarded.

The beret and its badge were minutely inspected. Each badge shone in the morning light; but what of its back? "Take out your badges", came the order, and if its back had not been as highly polished as the front, no 'stick' for you that day. The officer ran his hand across your face and chin, and a single bristle which had escaped the morning shave would disqualify you. We even opened our mouths so that the cleanliness of our teeth could be examined.

In the Royal Tank Regiment we mounted guard not with rifles but revolvers, and we carried six small bullets in the holster, and the top of each had to be highly polished. So the process would continue, down to and including our boots. "Lift your feet!" was the final order, and we stood on one leg, like horses waiting to be shod by the blacksmith, so that the studs could be examined, because they must be brightly polished too. Proud was the day when I became stick-man, and returned to my squadron lines, hero for the day.

I did not distinguish myself quite so favourably one day on the weekly pay parade. We lined up in front of the table behind which sat the pay officers. As our number, rank and name were called we marched forward, saluted, picked up our pay, turned about, and marched away. I was rather proud of my regulation salute - "Longest way up, shortest way down" - and I brought up my right arm in a wide sweep which knocked the in-tray off the table. I apologised, picked up my pay, saluted again - and knocked down the out-tray. I much enjoyed watching the television series Some Mothers do 'ave 'Em, recognising a kindred spirit in the unfortunate Frank, so brilliantly played by Michael Crawford.

Army leaves were always enjoyable. When in London I spent much time with the Spanish friends whom I had met on my voyage home from South Africa. Blanca was at work by day, but I would go to her family's flat and await her arrival. Often only her old grandmother would be at home, and she spoke no word of English, so I had good practice in improving the Spanish I had begun to learn on my way to the Falkland Islands, and with which I had persevered in South Africa.

Blanca was a sweet and innocent girl, overwhelmed by London, and she loved me to show her its deceptively bright lights. After life in a Spanish village or Gibraltar, she thought it greatly daring to be out late at night in London, and would laughingly refer to us as los pdjaros de la noche: very happy night-birds enjoying shorts breaks from the rigour of Army life or the tedium of a wartime office.

I corresponded with her regularly, until I felt my written Spanish becoming better than hers, which would occasionally produce some amusing instances of that confusion of spelling and pronunciation characteristic of so many Spaniards. On one occasion she meant to ask me when I would next be coming to see her, but she became hopelessly lost in a maze of confusion between the Spanish "v" and "b", between "a" and a silent "h". So "a verme" - to see me - came out as "haberme" - to have me - which was not what Blanquita had in mind at all.

On a subsequent leave I went home to Pontypool, where I called on my fellow-member of British Union, Gwyn. It was intended to be a brief courtesy visit only, but it developed into a warm romance. We spent most of that and subsequent leaves together, sometimes in Pontypool or Monmouth, sometimes with friends in Birmingham, and at other times in London. Between leaves I used to lead a monastic life, saving every penny from my meagre Army pay, so as to be able to enjoy the high life on my next leave. We used to stay at a particularly select hotel, frequented by the highest-ranking officers of the three services. As we entered restaurant or bar, packed with admirals, brigadiers, and air-marshals, every head would turn. Gwyn was strikingly beautiful, and was a magnet for all male eyes, but I received some attention too. Who was this intruder, this outsider bearing not the King's Commission, but a folded beret pushed through the epaulette on the shoulder of his ill-fitting uniform, which bore not even the single stripe of that unloved character, the provisional, unpaid lance-corporal? We loved to stand at the bar and feel the hostile stares boring into our backs. It may have embarrassed the rest of the company, but we carried it off with great aplomb.

This romance survived several leaves, but cooled off under the handicap of long separations, so finally we settled for a relationship of 'just good friends'. Gwyn carried me a further step along the path to Rome, and she was happy when she heard that I had been received into her Catholic church. I was stationed near Maidstone at the time, and I made my profession of faith in the town's delightful little neo-Gothic church of St. Francis of Assisi, on the Feast of the Epiphany, 1944.

My final Army posting took me to Northumberland, to a camp near Rothbury, from which we used to travel once a week to the pithead baths at Ashington, there to perform our ablutions, in Army phraseology. I kept up my cross-country running, and one day I took part in a particularly gruelling race around Blyth. It drained me completely. Afterwards, as I sat in a cafe, ashen-faced, sunk in depression, two cheerful Geordie lasses came over to my table. They aroused me from my apathy and banished my suicidal thoughts, and looked after me for the rest of my stay in the area. They even tried to persuade me to settle in the north-east when my Army career came to an end, but when that time came I took the road to London instead.

I left the Army in a fashion almost as bizarre as that of my entry. I was on guard duty one day when a relief was brought out from the guard-room and I was told to parade before the commanding officer. I presented myself and learned he had received orders, without a word of explanation, that I was to be discharged! There was no time to issue me with a complete set of civilian clothes, so I left for London wearing a demob suit with my khaki Army shirt and Army boots. The suit had been made by the tailoring firm of Schneider. It had not exactly been made to measure and was in fact so ill-fitting that I christened it my 'Schneider Trophy', after the famous air-race award of the thirties. A comrade gave me his mother's address, and she took me under her wing until I could get my bearings and settle down in civvy street again.

The whole affair was an absurdity, with no rational explanation. The sole charge preferred against me had been dismissed, so my discharge papers recorded: "Military conduct: Very Good". Yet the reason for discharge was recorded as: His Majesty has no further use for his services. Only my political boffin could have thought of sacking a man because he was very good!

I wrote to the War Office to ask why exactly I had been discharged, and to ask if I might be recalled. The reply read: "The reasons for your discharge are those stated on your discharge papers, namely: 'His Majesty has no further use for your services.' It is not proposed to recall you for further service." I have never pursued the matter.

So I survived my several years in the Army and emerged from my varied military career with my political beliefs unchanged, but with a deeper understanding of my fellow-men. They had not been wasted years.

Chapter Twelve

When I left the Army, London was being subjected to the first attacks from flying-bombs and rockets. In the isolated areas where tanks were stationed the war had largely passed us by. The brunt of the enemy's onslaught had been borne by London and other great cities, as I was now to witness at close range. However, I had had a glimpse of enemy action while in the Army and stationed at Hythe. German planes would come over of an evening, skimming over the waves from France in the deepening dusk, so that they were scarcely visible. As the sirens sounded we were supposed to run up to the roof of the house in which we were billeted and man an anti-aircraft gun. By the time we reached the gun the Luftwaffe had dashed over Hythe and shot-up the marshalling yards in the railway sidings at Ashford, and then turned tail and headed back to France. Occasionally we were in time to spot the enemy disappearing over the Channel, in the direction of the French coast, clearly visible from Hythe in good weather. In fact, the view was often so clear that we could pick out German army vehicles moving up and down the coast. But I saw and heard much more of the war after reaching London.

Wartime conscription had produced an acute shortage of teachers, and I was invited to attend the Ministry of Education for an interview, with a view to re-entering the profession. The invitation stipulated that I must be prepared to undergo a medical examination, and "a written examination in English"; but on my document the latter requirement had been crossed out. As I sat in the waiting-room I watched two Central European refugees struggling to write an essay, no doubt in order to satisfy the Ministry that they had sufficient command of our language to teach in an English school. When I overheard one candidate ask the other how to spell "skintillating", I thought

121

my chances of selection must be good, and so it proved. My interviewer was impressed by my teaching record in State and private schools, and in the Falkland Islands, and he asked me if I would be prepared to attend a twelve-month refresher course at a teachers' training college. I readily agreed, and I was assured that I would receive confirmation of my acceptance within a few days. Instead, I received a curt postcard telling me that I had "not been considered suitable". The Ministry of Education also had its political boffin.

A friend in London rented me a room, and I started to look for work. The employment exchange in the area, Willesden, had a vacancy for an assistant to the Personnel Manager of Park Royal Coachworks, lately part of the tottering British Leyland empire. The most apt of all clichés is surely the saying that truth is stranger than fiction. In that factory I witnessed scenes that would have been dismissed as too fantastic if they had been included in such a film as I'm All Right, Jack. The Personnel Manager was an old Harrovian, with a public school charm somewhat wasted on the shop stewards of North London's industrial belt. They bombarded our offices with complaints, and memories of my teaching days at Lewes came flooding back, because here too there was no polite knock on the door, but more likely a kick to send it flying open. Two shop stewards would enter and advance on the manager in a highly threatening manner.

There would be much angry and confused shouting before they stormed out again, with threats of dire action unless they obtained 'justice' immediately. I was anxious to pick up the political threads again and I thought the best way to go about it would be to see what was going on at Speaker's Corner, in Hyde Park. So there I went on my first free Sunday afternoon, and came across a meeting at which a former member of British Union was denouncing Defence Regulation 18B and internment without trial. He must have been a man of enormous courage to stand up and take this line before a mainly hostile audience of organised opposition, while the war was still on.

In the audience I discovered another ex-member, who outlined to me an interesting plan. During his internment he had met a James Taylor who had broken away from the British Legion and formed his own 'League of Ex-Servicemen. 'Why should we not join this organisation and campaign for ex-service rights, while extending its platform to include a defence of Mosley, and to prepare for his return to active politics?

I was happy to support the idea, and soon we had attracted a few kindred spirits. We met regularly, and discussed the plan in detail: in too much detail, because it became bogged down in pointless discussion of trivial matters, such as the type of office furniture we should require, what heading our writing-paper should carry, etc., when in fact we had no office, nor any hope of acquiring one.

I was reluctant to challenge the views of men who had been more active and prominent in British Union than I, but my instinct told me that no progress would ever be made unless discussion were translated into action. So one day I took a portable platform to the corner of Edgware Road and Star Street, mounted it, and made the first outdoor speech of my life. A crowd gathered out of curiosity, and at the end of my speech I got off the platform and passed around a tin for a collection. I then got on to the platform again and invited questions. This unusual solo effect attracted some support from former British Union members and others, who urged me to start meetings in the movement's old and traditional strongholds in East London. I agreed, and the first meetings were held on Sunday mornings in Bethnal Green, followed by Sunday evening meetings at Ridley Road, Dalston.

We decided to expand both the name and the scope of the organisation, which became The British League of Ex-servicemen and Women, as we aimed at attracting recruits from women who had been in the services. It was, throughout, a genuine ex-service organisation, and I learned to represent ex-service men and women in appeals to Pensions Tribunals where

Chapter Twelve

I won several cases. The British League also served to keep the
name of Sir Oswald Mosley before the public at a time when
he was restricted by the conditions imposed upon him after his
release from internment. (He was released only when his health
had so deteriorated that his life was endangered. The Communist
Party mounted a 'Put Mosley Back in Gaol' campaign, to which
the government refused to bow).

Mosley was farming at Ramsbury in Wiltshire, and from there
he produced a monthly Mosley News Letter, commenting on
current affairs. In 1946 he published his first post-war book, My
Answer, largely a reprint of his pre-war Tomorrow We Live, with
a new introduction confirming that he stood by all he had said
and written between the 1914 and 1939 wars. His ideas had been
right at the time, and have been proved to be so by the subsequent
course of events. This has been acknowledged by a number of
leading figures. In his English History, 1914-1945, published in
1965, the historian A.J.P. Taylor wrote that Mosley's proposals
"offered a blueprint for most of the constructive advances in
economic policy to the present day", and Michael Foot, writing
in the Evening Standard of 22 October 1968, said that "What
Mosley so valiantly stood for could have saved his country
from the Hungry Thirties and the horrors of the Second World
War." Mosley's first real post-war book was The Alternative,
published in 1947. It made clear that he now regarded the too
narrow nationalism of pre-war fascism as obsolete, and he
advocated an advance to a post-war creed of European union.
Both My Answer and The Alternative were boycotted by the
book trade, so ways and means had to be devised to overcome
this obstacle. Book clubs were established by some of Mosley's
old and new friends throughout the country. Two of these I was
able to organise myself, one in West London, where I lived, and
another in East London, where I was most politically active.

Inspired by the example of the bold anti-18B speaker I too held
a meeting in Hyde Park, and encountered violent opposition,
reported in the next morning's papers. I used to start work in

the factory an hour later than the shop-floor workers, and when I arrived I found that the communists had laid on a reception committee for me. They had threatened the personnel manager with sticks and stones, with which they said they would break all his office windows, and possibly him too, if I were not instantly sacked. The manager was waiting for me at the factory gate, with my insurance cards and a week's wages in lieu of notice in his hand. I protested that there were no grounds whatever for dismissing me. This he did not dispute, but instead he raised his bid. Would I go quietly for two weeks' wages, or three? I accepted one or the other, and left. Unfortunately, there were no industrial tribunals in those days, so I could not appeal for substantial compensation for wrongful dismissal.

I returned to my lodgings and told my landlady that the factory had asked me to leave, and she replied: "So am I!" I packed my bags, found new lodgings, and moved in. On the following Sunday afternoon I spoke in Hyde Park again, and on the Monday morning the newspapers carried reports of the meeting. The same evening my new landlady gave me notice and I moved out at the end of the week. For four consequent weekends I suffered the same ordeal, and I was about to sleep rough when a friend took pity on me and allowed me the use of a room in his flat. The Willesden Employment Exchange suggested that I should move out of the 'Red belt' of North London's industrial area, and the manager gave me a letter of introduction to the Marylebone Exchange. There I was provided with a somewhat unusual job as book-keeper to a firm of millinery manufacturers. Although not involved in the creative side of the business I became something of an authority on ladies' hats, ribbons, and ornamental trimmings.

One evening I rashly ventured into Hyde Park alone and started asking questions at a communist meeting. Suddenly I was attacked from behind, and found myself surrounded by a hostile mob, who began punching, kicking and howling abuse. It was obviously an occasion for making a strategic withdrawal, so I fought my way out of the park, around the Marble Arch, and across the road to the corner of Park Lane. There I was able to get my back against the railings of the underground station, so that I could concentrate on fighting off the frontal attacks.

Two policemen fought their way through the mob, but they became trapped themselves, pinioned against the railings on either side of me, too tightly hemmed in to draw their truncheons. Eventually a police van arrived with reinforcements, and we jumped in and were driven off to Marylebone Lane police station. The fight had not been conducted strictly according to Queensberry rules, and I was in a considerably dishevelled condition, with most of my jacket and shirt buttons missing. Grateful for the police assistance, I dropped a small donation into a police widows' and orphans' box, while the exhausted officers unbuttoned their tunics and recovered their breath over cups of tea.

With demobilisation the number of ex-servicemen and women increased, and recruitment for The British League was brisk. We were able to hold many more meetings. Our speeches and the meetings themselves provoked allegations and counter-allegations, charges and counter-charges, of violence and anti-Semitism. The air seemed to be as thick with them as it was with the missiles of our opponents. These accusations should be looked at objectively, now that the heat of battle is over and the dust has subsided. I dealt with the matter in an article which I was invited to write for the *Acton Gazette*, and which appeared in that paper on 5 January 1978. In it I said: 'Anti-Semitism? We have never attacked any man on grounds of race or religion. We clashed with some Jews in the thirties because of our opposition to the threatened war with Germany, which we did not consider to be in British interests. In the immediate post-war years I felt it my duty as an ex-serviceman to protest against the flogging and hanging of British soldiers in Palestine . . .

A group of Jews attacked me on a number of occasions, once knocking me unconscious and putting me into hospital with a blow from a flying brick. Some time ago I was stopped in South Parade by a man who told me he had been a member of that group.

We agreed that it was now ancient history, and I was deeply touched when he held out his hand, which I readily accepted. Let me now put the clock back over forty years and try to add some flesh to the bare bones of that statement. In the thirties we appreciated the concern of British Jews at the fate of their fellows in Germany, but we resented their attacks on our essentially British fascist movement, and their attempts to involve Britain in a war against Germany. Some post-war Jews professed to see in our British League meetings a 'revival of fascism', although we were at pains to make it clear that we regarded the fascist era as closed, and believed that new policies were essential to meet the new problems of the post-war world. Copies of Mosley's *The Alternative* were on sale at our meetings, and if our opponents had taken the trouble to read and study it they would have understood that we had advanced beyond fascism to Europeanism.

The issue was complicated by the question of Palestine. We were not the first to criticise British governments which perpetuated the first World War policy of promising Palestine to both Jews and Arabs, a policy which involved the British Army in the hopeless task of endeavouring to keep the peace between the rival claimants, and in being attacked by both.

In any national struggle the nationalists see their men and women as heroes and heroines, martyrs for the cause, and they condone any efforts to secure the desired end. But to other eyes the same men and women appear as terrorists, steeped in the blood of innocent victims. Mr. Begin, now the Prime Minister of Israel, certainly condoned, even if he did not actually order, the flogging and hanging of British soldiers. Over this matter I exercised my right of protest, speaking from the roof of a loud-speaker van, at Sunday night meetings at Ridley Road, Dalston, and elsewhere.

Chapter Twelve

Some Jews claimed the right to silence me by any methods, so fierce clashes were inevitable. I once described an incident of this kind to a friend as "a fair fight", but when I elaborated on the methods and weapons used against me he said that he thought "an unfair fight" would be a more apt description.

The police in East and North London were called upon to perform a similar role to that of the British Army in Palestine, albeit a less dangerous one. They had to try to keep the peace and enforce the law, bringing all who offended against it before the courts. At first most of those arrested at our meetings were opponents of British League, and they often emerged from the courts with a small fine or no penalty at all, because they pleaded that they "just happened to be passing by the meeting" and had been "provoked" by the speaker's remarks, which they claimed were highly insulting. The matter was eventually tested in the courts, in a case which was blown up out of all proportion and became something of a cause celebre.

Rival organisations, ranging from the Communist Party to AJEX (the Association of Jewish Ex-Servicemen) tried to bring our meetings to a halt by 'jumping the pitch', as the police worked on the principle of first come, first served. Competition for the best street-corners reached absurd lengths, with platforms concealed under stalls in Ridley Road's Saturday market. As the stalls closed down the platform would go up, and a speaker would open a meeting, perhaps at 5p.m. on a Saturday. He would obviously not speak continuously, but if challenged by a rival organisation he would go through the motions of addressing an invisible audience, even at two or three o'clock on a Sunday morning. But if he were caught napping, another organisation might well open its meeting on the site, and call on the police to disperse the supplanted rivals.

We had a specialist at this game of cat-and-mouse in 'Jock' Holliwell, so named because he did not have a drop of Scottish blood in his veins. Early on Sunday morning he would saunter into Ridley Road, carrying an innocent-looking brown-paper parcel, which in fact contained a brick. If our rivals were resting against a wall, or at an all-night coffee-stall, he would put down his brick, step on to it, and announce in a loud voice: "I declare open this British League meeting!"

In the early months of 1947 there appeared to be a lull in the opposition's activities, and I thought it safe to divide our forces. I left a skeleton crew to hold a meeting at Ridley Road while I went on to open a new pitch in Tottenham. But opposition intelligence had been good, and our opponents turned up in force at Ridley Road, where they closed down our meeting, and then dashed up to Tottenham. In a clash there I was arrested, and charged with using "insulting words and behaviour." When the case was heard I was solemnly bound over "to keep the peace with all His Majesty's lawful subjects and to be of good behaviour for a period of twelve calendar months." Later, more serious matters were to come before the courts.

In describing what became known as 'The Battle of Ridley Road' I shall quote from the pamphlet of that title by my dear friend the late Alexander Raven Thomson, known to us all as 'Raven'. He has been described as "the philosopher of British fascism." He had been educated at Scots, German and American universities, where he had studied philosophy, and in 1932 he published his book Civilisation as Divine Superman, on the ideas of the German philosopher Oswald Spengler, author of The Decline of the West. In Spengler's view the decay of western civilisation could be prevented only by replacing our individualistic capitalism with some form of collectivist State structure.

This line of thought had taken Raven into the Communist Party, but he did not remain there long. He rejected the materialistic interpretation of history, and from collectivism he moved on to a corporist view of the State. He then recognised in Oswald Mosley a leader whom he could follow, and he joined British Union in

1933. He remained with us in the post-war Union Movement until his too-early death in 1955, working in his office until he was found collapsed on the floor, a victim of the cancer which later killed him.

He was that rare combination of theorist and philosopher and fine open-air speaker, fearless in the face of violent opposition. I can see him now, in my mind's eye, jacket off, shirt sleeves rolled up, quelling all opposition with his command of language and his powerful voice. In My Life Mosley wrote: "Intellectually Raven Thomson towered above the men I had known in the Labour Cabinet of 1929, and in firmness of character he seemed in an altogether different category to most contemporary politicians... He died young, and we his friends will always feel that the prison years and the decline of his country combined to curtail a life which would have been of brilliant service to the nation."

In The Battle of Ridley Road, Raven quoted from an article in the Sunday Pictorial of 17 August 1947 by the journalist Frederick Mullally, author of the book Fascism Inside England. In this article, referring to British League meetings, Mullally wrote that "thugs with the eyes of morons and faces of gorillas sold Mosley pamphlets like hot cakes among the crowd"; scarcely a flattering description of my friends. He continued: 'Okay, Hamm, let us see the stuff you and your audiences are made of. I'm coming down to Ridley Road again — tonight. I'm going to ask for the use of your microphone for just ten minutes. I know you can dish it out. Let's see if you can take it.'

Let Raven continue the story. After recording that I had decided to accede to Mullally's request, with the proviso that if he were given access to my platform I should be allowed some space in his Sunday Pictorial column, the pamphlet continues: 'Unfortunately, this offer could not be made, as Mr. Mullally saw fit to go first to a communist meeting to collect a bodyguard and then drove suddenly into the League meeting at the head of his supporters. Very naturally, disorder resulted and Mr Mullally was grasped by the beard and hurled to the ground, and the perfectly orderly meeting he had rudely interrupted dissolved in confusion. Then came strange police decisions. Instead of arresting the interrupter and permitting the meeting to proceed, the police rescued Mr. Mullally from his ignominious discomfiture and escorted him to a neighbouring street, where he addressed his bedraggled bodyguard under police protection. Meanwhile, they ordered the League meeting to close down, with the result that the indignant audience proceeded to the communist meeting, where they smashed the platform and carried off the local party banner in triumph.' The 'Battle of Ridley Road' continued to rage every Sunday evening until a combination of circumstances brought it to an end, with complete victory for us, in mid-October 1947.

At its height I experienced a somewhat traumatic weekend, from 12 to 14 September. My employer had received threatening letters from a Jewish organisation known as the 43 Group, and on the Friday I left him, with a week's pay in lieu of notice, a procedure which was becoming a habit. On the Saturday morning I was returning to my flat from a morning walk when I noticed a police car outside the door. A Special Branch inspector was waiting to serve me with a summons charging me with having used 'insulting words and behaviour' at Ridley Road the previous Sunday. Attached to the summons were some extracts from the offending speech. The inspector warned me that if I were to use similar expressions at any meetings held before the hearing of the summons, I would be arrested.

The serving of this summons was reported in the next day's newspapers, and an exceptionally large crowd gathered at Ridley Road that evening. I finished my speech, and then climbed down the ladder at the back of the loudspeaker van. But before my feet could touch the ground I was seized round the waist by my irate inspector, and was almost thrown into a police van, under arrest. He seemed almost speechless with rage, but eventually I could make out that he was saying, somewhat incoherently: "You said it again! You said it again!" At last he managed to tell me what the offending words were: my description of our opponents as "pale, pink, palpitating pansies" — the kind of expression, not over-nice or accurate, perhaps, that any public orator is likely to use under constant taunting by a hostile audience. It seemed that I had used the same colourful phrase the previous Sunday, and that it had been among the extracts from my speech attached to the summons. I assured the Inspector that I had not noticed it — for I had given the extracts only a cursory glance — and had not repeated it as an act of defiance, or to insult him personally, but his only comment was: "You've done it now!" I was taken to Hackney police station in Dalston Lane, where I was charged in the same terms as on the previous day's summons, under Section 5 of the Public Order Act of 1936. I was released on bail to appear at North London Magistrates' Court the following morning, my birthday.

Police station charge rooms have witnessed many moments of light relief, and I made my own humble contribution that Sunday evening. When asked to turn out my pockets I placed on the counter a pile of railway tickets to Brighton. I had organised a British League meeting at Brighton for the following week, and I had bought the tickets at a reduced party rate, for distribution to my friends and supporters.

There were at that time three stipendiary magistrates sitting at the North London court, one of whom I had already met, under rather unusual circumstances. I had been speaking one Sunday lunchtime at the Whitestone Pond on Hampstead Heath, and I had noticed at the back of the crowd an elderly man shaking his stick at my vociferous hecklers, and defending me in a loud voice. After the meeting I learned that he was one of the three wise men who sat in judgement on the North London bench. I now wondered if it might be my good fortune to appear before him on the Monday morning, but when I appeared I was a little disconcerted to see instead Magistrate No. 2. I did not really suspect him of prejudice, but let us say that his political opinions, which he sometimes expressed in public, did not quite coincide with my own, or those of Magistrate No. 1. But he was exquisitely polite, inquiring whether it would be 'convenient' to me if the two cases against me were heard at the same time. With equal politeness and old-world courtesy I assured him that the arrangement would suit me admirably. So the hearing was fixed for Saturday, 18 October.

We decided to make a test case of this ridiculous affair, and I went to the well-known firm of solicitors Fearnley-Whittingstall, where I saw the head of the firm and asked him to brief his brother, a leading counsel of the period, to defend me. The solicitor and his clerk started taking notes, when they referred to their diaries and discovered that both brothers were likely to be abroad on the date set for the hearing. They were going to Palestine, as it then was, to defend Captain Roy Farran, who had been charged with the murder of a young Jew. The case against him collapsed, and they would have been back in time for my case, but they had already passed the brief to a Mr. Neville Faulks, who later became a High Court judge. The Farran case had a tragic sequel. Roy Farran was sent back to England after the case, to avoid the vengeance of the Stem Gang. Sometime later a parcel arrived at his home, addressed to 'R. Farran, Esq.', and his brother Rex opened it in error. It contained a bomb, which blew off his hands and killed him.

A conference was arranged with Mr. Faulks, at which we discussed in detail the transcript of my speech, which had been obtained from the Special Branch shorthand writers present at all my meetings. In one passage I had described Prime Minister Clement Attlee as "the sort of man who enters a room in such a way that you think someone has gone out." Mr. Faulks commented that he knew of a better description: Mr. Attlee reminded him of "a pianist in a brothel, strumming away on the keys without a clue as to what was going on upstairs."

On the day of the hearing the presiding magistrate was the third of the trio, Mr. Blake Odgers, then an unknown quantity. There was such a queue outside the court that one would have thought there was at least a murder trial in progress. A newspaper reported that a dear old lady passing by asked what the queue was for, and was told: "They've got Hamm inside." It was in the days of post-war food rationing, and she hopefully fumbled in her bag for her ration book.

The Inspector who had arrested me gave his evidence, and suggested that my speech had been so provocative that "the crowd was in a frenzy." In a long and highly skilled cross-examination Mr. Faulks tried to elicit from the Inspector what particular sentences in my speech had had this extraordinary effect. Could it have been one of my many references to the pre-war British Empire, "that glorious Empire on which the sun never sets", whose demise I had lamented? Did not such passages remind the Inspector of the Sunday Express? "I don't know", came the reply, "I never read the Sunday Express." Might not another passage have been written by Lord Beaverbrook himself? Again came the reply: "I don't know. I've never heard of Lord Beaverbrook."

The Inspector was gently led into the trap which counsel had skilfully laid for him, and at last he blurted out: "Hamm's mere presence at Ridley Road is enough to cause a riot!" This was basically true, since the opposition was highly organised and would have been 'in a frenzy' if I had merely recited nursery rhymes. Mr. Faulks quietly observed: "I'm inclined to agree with you, Inspector. But my client is charged with using insulting words and behaviour, not with having an insulting face!"

The proceedings had their inevitable lighter side. In another purple passage I had waxed eloquent about "the Greek ideal, expressed in the Roman maxim mens sana in corpore sano." The Special Branch's highly efficient shorthand writers, who often had to work under very difficult conditions, always did their best to take down every word correctly. We had a mutual understanding that if I were carried away as the adrenalin flowed, and started to speak too fast for them, they would signal to me to slow down, and I would do so. On this occasion, however, they had missed a few vital words and the passage in question came out as "the Greek maxim mens sana in corpore sano. " The magistrate politely inquired whether I knew the difference between Greek and Latin. When I assured him that I did, and explained what had happened, he nodded with appreciative understanding. I felt that we had moved from the court into the more friendly atmosphere of the Senior Common Room. In fact, by the time the defence had closed its case the whole matter had almost been laughed out of court.

I felt some sympathy for the magistrate, who was obviously anxious to dismiss both charges, yet was reluctant to upset the Home Office, which undoubtedly had inspired the prosecution, under pressure from constant deputations from my political opponents. He spent about twenty minutes trying to draw a subtle distinction between the two charges, when none was clearly visible to the naked eye. I used to make basically the same speech, with some variation of content, week after week. There had been no hint of prosecution on the many previous occasions, and Special Branch officers had always been present. However, the magistrate managed to reach a happy compromise by dismissing one charge and finding the other proven. Justice had not only been done, but had been seen to have been done. He bound me over to keep the peace, after tactfully omitting to ask if I had any previous convictions.

The fact that I was already bound over would have made the affair much more serious, with imprisonment almost inevitable. There was a flurry in court as the Inspector rushed to the witness-box to remind the magistrate of his omission. But Mr. Blake Odgers had the last word: "You are too late, Inspector", he announced with a charming smile. "I have already announced my decision, and I cannot change it now." I was driven by my supporters from the court to a nearby cafe, where the celebrations continued far into the night; a celebration of a victory for free speech and common sense. The following night there was a monster meeting at Ridley Road, described by Raven Thomson as "a mass celebration of the victory of freedom of speech, with the opposition strangely quiet, and an audience of thousands applauding what was undoubtedly one of the finest speeches ever made by Jeffrey Hamm in East London."

"The Battle of Ridley Road' had been fought and won. After all the excitement perhaps an anti-climax was inevitable. The organised opposition paraded once or twice outside North London court, carrying banners with the strange inscription' 'Blake Odgers is a Fascist.' But they stopped coming to Ridley Road in any numbers, and the exceptionally severe winter of 1947-48 eventually brought the meetings to an end: something the opposition had been unable to do. While my friends and I were making some contribution to Oswald Mosley's return to active politics, some former colleagues of his were pursuing a different course. They invited me to meet them, and I did so without prejudice, confident that they could never seduce me from my allegiance to Mosley. The first of these was John Beckett, the former Labour M.P. who had caused a sensation in the House of Commons by walking up to the Speaker's table and removing the mace, in emulation of Cromwell's "take away that bauble." He had left British Union and parted from Mosley when the latter had expelled William Joyce; together they had formed the National Socialist League, which collapsed with the outbreak of war and Joyce's departure for Germany. Over lunch, Beckett presented a mildly plausible anti-Mosley case, but my faith remained unshaken.

I never met William Joyce, but I had heard him speak at British Union meetings. He was a highly gifted speaker, but inclined to take a perverse delight in antagonising an audience, with heavy scorn and sarcasm, rather than attempting to win them over. But his wit and repartee were proverbial. On one occasion a buxom lady in the crowd was shouting abuse at him, culminating in an angry roar: "You bastard!" Quick as a flash Joyce gave her a cheerful wave, as he cried: "Hullo, Mother!"

Mosley's post-war opponents tried to make political capital out of Joyce's execution for treason. This was manifestly absurd, as Joyce's wartime broadcasts from Germany were made two years and more after Mosley had expelled him from British Union, for his anti-Semitism and disloyalty. No reasonable person would hold Mosley responsible for Joyce's subsequent behaviour. So Joyce became a mild political nuisance to us, and it is difficult to defend the actions of a man who professed great loyalty to Britain, but went on to broadcast for her enemies in wartime. But was he guilty of treason, and should he have been hanged?

The defence at his trial proved conclusively that he was an Irish American, who therefore owed no allegiance to the British Crown once he was outside its jurisdiction, in Germany. Nor had he committed any offence under American law, as he had become a naturalised German before America entered the war. The prosecution relied on the dubious argument that if a man travelled on a British passport, which in Joyce's case he had undoubtedly obtained illegally, he thereby owed allegiance to the British Crown. His appeal went to the House of Lords, where one law lord gave a dissenting judgement in favour of allowing the appeal. The other noble lords rejected the appeal and Joyce was hanged.

I separated my political objections to Joyce from my uneasiness over his conviction and fate, and I was with his brother and sister and a few of his friends during his execution. I lunched on several occasions with A.K. Chesterton, author of the pre-war biography of Mosley, Portrait of a Leader. He too had parted company with Mosley, and they drifted further apart in the post-war years. Chesterton wallowed in nostalgia for a British Empire which no longer existed, and founded a League of Empire Loyalists. Mosley meanwhile had founded Union Movement, to advance the concept of a united Europe to replace the lost Empire. Chesterton wined and dined me, and entertained me with further mildly plausible attacks on Mosley, but he too completely failed to convince me.

Chapter Twelve

The then Duke of Bedford, father of the present Duke, had formed a British People's Party, with John Beckett as his secretary. He was an amiable character, and had opposed the second World War with considerable courage. I met him on a number of occasions, but I was never tempted to join any organisation which rejected Oswald Mosley and his ideas.

In this period I was the victim of two physical attacks. At the Brighton meeting which I have mentioned I was knocked down and kicked, but I successfully warded off a razor attack and gave the matter no further thought. I was living at the time in a rather primitive basement flat, with no electricity, so I undressed in the dark that night. It was light when I awoke and dressed, and it was only then that I discovered that the seat of my trousers had been badly razor-slashed. Fortunately, I had sustained no injury.

On another occasion, when I was living in a third-floor flat in a house in North Kensington, there was a knock at my door one Saturday night, and I opened it. I thought I recognised several well known members of the 43 Group, but before I could close the door, or take any evasive action, I was hit in the face with a knuckle-duster with such force that I was thrown across the room and into the fireplace. I thought I recognised my principal assailant at a meeting the following morning, and I asked a police officer to take his name and address so that I could take out a summons against him for assault.

The case was heard at West London Magistrates' Court, and a man from the flat below mine gave evidence. We had a system, known to our friends, of heavy knocks on the front door of the house to indicate who was wanted, as the doorbell seemed to be permanently out of order. The code was two knocks for the man on the second floor, and three for me on the third. My neighbour below had heard what sounded like two knocks, and had gone down to open the front door, where he found several men on the step.

One of them, he deposed, had asked for "Jeffrey", so he had

allowed them to go upstairs. Suddenly he had heard a commotion, and had come back out of his room to see what the matter was, when he was brushed aside by men running down the stairs and out into the street to a waiting car. "As I came to court today," he told the magistrate, "I saw on the step the man who had asked for 'Jeffrey' — and there he is now!" And he pointed to the man in the dock.

He was an entirely independent witness, with no interest in politics, and the magistrate congratulated him on the wisdom of this attitude, and on the clarity and precision with which he had given his evidence. The court then adjourned. At the resumed hearing some weeks later the defence produced a 'perfect alibi', in the form of a night-club members' book, which 'proved' that my assailant had been there the whole evening in question. I reminded the magistrate of his favourable comments on my witness and his evidence, but he replied that the witness "must have been mistaken." The case was dismissed, and I was ordered to pay costs! These were immediately paid for me by indignant members of the public in the gallery. They had taken a collection, to which one of the police officers who had been in court was seen to contribute. Perhaps the case illustrates how unreliable may be evidence of identification.

We must always endeavour to learn from our mistakes. Since that day I do not put my head forward when I open the door to any knock or ring. I step back until I have clearly established the identity of my visitor. This precaution, and others such as standing well away from the kerb in bus queues, or from the edge of railway platforms, may have prolonged my life in this age of political violence.

I cannot leave this transition period and move on to the real post-war years without recalling one more 'character'. During my years in Harrow and my membership of the local branch of British Union I had formed a close friendship with the late Father Clement Lloyd Russell, whose church lay between Harrow and Sudbury. He was an ardent supporter of Mosley and his movement. At the time of his reception into the Catholic Church he had been an Anglican curate, and he remained very English, with a grave suspicion of any of his fellow priests who had been educated in Rome. Successive Archbishops of Westminster were dismissed with a deprecatory gesture and a contemptuous "Of course, he's a Rome man."

Photographs of Mosley and other British Union personalities, resplendent in Blackshirt uniform, adorned his mantle-piece, and I was curious to know what effect this might have had upon a new Archbishop who had just made his episcopal visit to the church. I telephoned to inquire: "Father, what did the Archbishop have to say about your art gallery?" "Not a word", was the reply, "he was speechless!"

I spent a delightful evening with him on one Army leave during the war, but I was mystified when he looked at his watch and quietly commented to his assistant priest: "Evening prayers, Father." What strange ceremony was this, to which I had not been initiated? My unspoken question was answered when the young priest crossed the room and switched on the radio. "Gairmany calling, Gairmany calling", announced William Joyce. This incident in no way implied German sympathies on the part of the patriotic and indeed intensely nationalist Father Russell, but was typical of his sense of fun and delight in teasing.

Another example of this was his quiet amusement in watching the dear fur-coated Tory matrons of his parish, patriotic to the core, singing the Tantum Ergo at Benediction to the tune of the German national anthem "Deutschland uber Alles", at the height of the war.

On Saturday, 15 November 1947, an historic meeting was held at the Memorial Hall in Farringdon Street, in the city. Fifty-one diverse organisations, including British League and the Mosley Book Clubs, came together to appeal to Sir Oswald Mosley to return to active politics and to found a new, post-war movement. Raven Thomson reported all the speeches in Mosley News Letter No. 13, of December 1947.

Of my personal appeal to Mosley he wrote: 'Jeffrey Hamm then spoke from the gallery, where he was surrounded by his most ardent League members from East London. Received with great enthusiasm, he spoke of the great struggle for freedom of speech which had been won for East London at Ridley Road. He now offered to merge the British League in a new movement under Mosley's leadership, and to support the new movement in any new capacity to which he was called.' Another phase of my life was over, and yet another was about to begin.

Chapter Thirteen

This book was not intended to be a political treatise, but rather one of personal recollections of life and politics, and of the interesting characters I have met therein. However, in the remaining chapters the emphasis will be chiefly on politics, and I shall have little to say about my private and domestic life. This is merely applying to myself the rigid rule I have observed towards all my political friends and acquaintances.

For example, I often said in the years when I was responsible for organising public meetings: "If a speaker appeared on our platform drunk (no one ever did) that would be my business. But if after a meeting a speaker went home and there got drunk, that would be his private affair, and no business of mine. Nor would it be my business whether he then went to bed with his wife, the wife of the man next door, or with another man."

I am a tolerant person, and on all such controversial issues, from alcoholism to adultery or homosexuality, I wholeheartedly subscribe to the French maxim: Chacun à son goût. In earlier chapters I have dealt lightly with the broken romances which strew many a young man's path through life. I did not take any of these rebuffs too seriously, and I did not die young of a broken heart. I sympathised with the poor girls who felt that they could not stand the pace of riotous public meetings, appearances in court, and other factors in my public life. I was able to laugh heartily with the charming Cheltenham nurse who told me, in the polished accents of that most respectable spa, that while she was quite fond of me, "My people would not approve of my marrying a destitute Fascist."

My wife-to-be accepted my life-style, a more realistic attitude than that of a girl convinced that she could change the character of a man set in his ways and determined to plough his own furrow, however rough and barren the soil. My son Peter and my daughter Paulina probably regard me as rather eccentric, but we tolerate each others idiosyncrasies. I have never tried to force my views on them, nor have I expected them to agree with me. I was sad when I had to neglect them for long periods in their childhood, under extreme pressure of work, but I made every possible effort to attend all functions, both academic and sporting, at their respective schools.

My son went to the Salesian College at Battersea, where his chief claim to fame was the setting of a school record for the mile, which stood for years after he had left. My daughter set an extraordinary record of being never absent, never late, on a single day between starting school at the age of five and leaving at eighteen. She did well academically at the Convent of the Sacred Heart, Hammersmith, with her ten "O" levels and four "A" levels, but she was much more proud of being Games Secretary in her penultimate year, and Games Captain in her final year. We treasure a photograph of her standing with a school friend and holding aloft between them three silver cups. Mary had won the Junior Tennis Singles, Paulina the netball shooting competition, and the two of them had won the Junior Tennis Doubles championship.

In her early years at Hammersmith Paulina's games mistress was the famous miler of that period, Anne Smith, coached by Gordon Pirie. After her controversial exclusion from the British Women's Athletics team for walking out of the European Games in Budapest (because Pirie was refused admission to the athletes' quarters) Anne had shown great strength of character by continuing to run as an individual competitor. I took Paulina and a bevy of Sacred Heart beauties to the Wimbledon track, where Anne set a new world's record for the mile, only to beat it a few weeks later at Chiswick. We followed her from track to track, and she was always encouraged by her girls and their shouts of "Come on, Miss!" When Anne left, her successor as games mistress persuaded me to umpire tennis matches, or to act as time-keeper at netball rallies, whenever I could spare the time until some of the girls thought I was a part-time member of the staff. There I will leave all family and personal matters and return to my political narrative.

Sir Oswald Mosley launched his post-war Union Movement at a conference in London on Saturday, 7 February, 1948. Its aims and objects are described and discussed at considerable length in its founder's autobiography and in the Robert Skidelsky biography. To me Union Movement meant, in essence, the political, economic and cultural union of all Europe, something going far beyond the purely economic and financial union to which the architects of the European Economic Community, or Common Market, aspired. This union of all Europe should go beyond the purely geographical Europe, and should include our former Dominions and also South Africa, to form a great 'third force' in the world, hostile to neither capitalist America nor to the communist bloc, but independent of both.

That vast, viable area, under the leadership of a European government, could be a powerful force for world peace. Its economic resources could provide its peoples with ever-rising living standards, and yield a surplus which could feed the hungry peoples of the world. This great act of humanity would lead to the collapse of communism, which thrives on the exploitation of human suffering and misery.

I was invited to join the office staff of Union Movement and handle the accounts, which I did during normal business hours. Our real work was carried on in the evenings and at weekends, at innumerable outdoor and indoor meetings. A detailed history of these would be tedious, and I shall mention the most important ones only, or those in which I was involved in some special way.

We had hoped to pay our small staff nominal salaries out of the collections taken up at meetings, but the virtual ending of outdoor meetings, both at Ridley Road and elsewhere by the severe winter weather (although they were resumed later, as stated above) soon made this impracticable. For months I augmented my own salary by selling morning newspapers outside Holland Park underground station for the owner of the pitch. He lived in East London, and by the time he arrived at Holland Park on the first train of the day he had missed the early morning trade. So I would be up at 5a.m. to meet the delivery van as it dumped the newspaper parcels on the pavement. With numbed fingers I would untie them and lay out my wares in time to catch the first commuters. But after a few months this burning of the candle at both ends proved too exhausting, and I was given a small rise to compensate for the loss of this additional income when I retired from the newsagents' trade.

All concerned with the launching of the new movement were unanimous in supporting the advance in policy beyond the narrow nationalism of Fascism to the wider concept of European union. But we had many long discussions on what other aspects of pre-war policies, strategy, tactics and methods should be preserved. For the movement's journal it was decided that Union was the most suitable name, and the first issue was published in February 1948. The pre-war 'flash and circle' symbol was retained, as it could now signify European action within European union, an advance on the pre-war British action within British union. The uniform, which in any case had never been worn by the mass membership, but only by those dedicated to almost nightly service to the movement, had been banned by the Public Order Act of 1936, and we had no desire to revive it, even if it had been lawful. Although the pre-war salute was Roman in origin, it too was abandoned on account of its association with Fascism.

Robert Skidelsky in his book Oswald Mosley argues that we did not break sufficiently with our pre-war past. He writes: "Indeed, the prevalence of the 'old guard' soon gave it a depressingly familiar look. Like the Bourbons, the fascists seemed to have learnt nothing and forgotten nothing." He goes on to suggest that my East London meetings led to a revival of "the quarrel with the Jews", but I trust I have disposed of this allegation in my description of 'The Battle of Ridley Road' and how it arose.

We certainly sought, and I personally perhaps least of all, no revival of that quarrel, strongly opposing any association with anti-Semites and other extremists, whose displeasure I have incurred by labelling them 'the lunatic fringe.' Yes, we did indeed turn to those of the 'old guard' who had remained loyal to Mosley, and we did march again through our old strongholds of East London, with flags flying high, and drums beating proudly. With hindsight, it may have been a tactical error, but we will never feel obliged to make any apology for it.

The most memorable meeting, in personal terms, at which I spoke in 1948 was held in Cephas Avenue, Mile End, on the evening of Wednesday, 1 September. Tommy Moran (a pre-war naval boxing champion) and his wife Toni were in London on holiday, and they spoke at a number of our meetings. On this particular evening I had opened a meeting for Toni, and while she was speaking the 43 Group arrived, and started stoning the loudspeaker van. Alf Flockhart, who was then the movement's assistant secretary, asked me to take over the meeting, and I climbed back on to the van, to face a barrage of missiles.

A police inspector began shouting to me from behind the van, calling on me to close the meeting, and threatening to come up and arrest me if I did not do so. It occurred to me that he would be taking his life in his hands if he climbed up beside me, under heavy fire, in his devotion to duty. I stalled him for some time, but he became increasingly insistent. It was then, as I mentioned in my opening chapter, that I forgot the golden rule of any ball game: never take your eye off the ball. I turned my head to call out to the inspector that I was just going to close the meeting, when I did so, but not in the conventional manner. I did not see the next flying missile, a brick which hit me on the side of the head, knocking me semi-unconscious. Then, as I learned later, the 43 Group rushed the van, and made it impossible for anyone to get me down while the battle raged below.

Among those fighting to defend the van (and his own life) was Len Adams, who later became a close friend of the late James Pope-Hennessy, historian and author of the official biography of Queen Mary. Len told me later that he had seen much wartime action as a paratrooper, and had never been frightened until that night. Attacked from all sides, as he swung his Army belt around his head in self-defence, he had hammered on a house door and pleaded for admission when an old lady opened it, "They're killing me, Ma", he had shouted, but she shut the door on him, terrified for her own safety. As it closed he had called to her: "All right, Ma, I'll die out here!"

Meanwhile, my head wound was bleeding profusely; the blood ran down a sleeve of my jacket, and down the side of the van, where its stains remained for some time as a souvenir of the fierce battle. The van was driven to Bethnal Green Hospital, with me lying on its roof. I was taken into the casualty ward, and my head stitched before I was put to bed.

Another old friend, Fred Bailey, told me an amusing tale later. He had climbed into the van and saw a car carrying 43 Group members following us. He had picked up some heavy object to throw at the car, to hamper its pursuit of us, but he hurled it with such force that he threw himself out too, almost under the wheels of the car. His wife-to-be had watched in horror, and had sent up an anguished cry of "My Freddie, my Freddie!" as he disappeared over the tailboard. Fortunately, he managed to roll clear of the car's wheels, and he lived to fight another day.

The injury made me very sick, and the next morning I felt ghastly. However, I revived somewhat when a kindly nurse told me that there was a letter for me. I opened it and read: "This time a brick, next time a bomb. If you speak again you will end up in the morgue. (Signed) The 43 Group." I thought this extremely kind and thoughtful of them. I was detained in hospital for four days and I had to take things quietly for some time, although I recall speaking at meetings with my head heavily bandaged.

I naturally ignored the 43 Group threat, and I continued to speak at meetings all over London. During this time I was also writing articles for Union, and in September of that year I began a series designed to summarise and simplify the contents of Mosley's book The Alternative.

Life continued in this manner until June 1949, when I was asked to move to Manchester to assist the local organiser, Philip Sutherst. I remained there for three years which I much enjoyed, and I still feel a strong affection for that city and its people. At first I stayed in lodgings in Moss Side, then a highly respectable area and not the ghetto into which it has now been turned by unrestricted immigration. My wife joined me after the birth of our son in August, and we went to live with friends in Prestwich. A little later we were able to buy, with locally raised funds, a property in Clowes Street, West Gorton, near Belle Vue, where we opened a Union Movement bookshop and lived above it.

I had not wished to involve my Moss Side landlord in political controversy, and he was happy in his belief that I was a free-lance journalist. The summer of 1949 was fine and warm, and I used to spend much of the day in Whitworth Park, portable typewriter on my knee, working on my series of articles on The Alternative. By September I had completed a summary of the whole book.

I had spoken in various parts of Manchester before I settled on Alexandra Park Gates, Moss Side, as my regular pitch. It had been for many years a regular 'Speakers' Corner' and the older men who gathered there each week, sitting on the park wall, could recall hearing Lloyd George, James Maxton and other famous figures of the past. I spoke there regularly, on Friday evenings and Sunday afternoons, so it required some ingenuity to think of something original to say at each meeting, with this hard core of friendly but critical experts in the audience on every occasion.

I also spoke in all the main Lancashire towns, and in many in Yorkshire, with meetings in Derby market place on alternate Sunday evenings. Here I would share the platform with Tommy Moran, a magnificent mob orator and a man of extraordinary physical courage. In his pre-war British Union days he had led a campaign in South Wales, challenging the communists in their strongholds in the Rhonnda valley. His face carried many a scar from these encounters, but they had earned him the respect even of his opponents.

In the afternoon they would overturn his platform and kick the prostrate Tommy before he could get to his feet and defend himself. He would go home and wash his wounds, before going into the town centre and into a pub where he knew his attackers would be drinking. They would then buy him a drink, assuring him: "You're a good man, Tommy, but you're on the wrong side."

Whenever an old newsreel of "The Battle of Cable Street' of October 1936 is shown on television Tommy's lone figure may be seen, surrounded by attackers whom he picked off one by one with straight lefts and rights, until felled from behind by a blow from a leg of a chair, around which barbed wire had been wrapped. He had been waylaid as he made his way to the assembly point for the march which never took place, and gave such a good account of himself that when he eventually collapsed in a pool of his own blood, opponents lay around him in a circle.

In September 1949 a particularly successful meeting in Bradford provoked the Yorkshire communists to lay on a warm reception committee for me when I returned a fortnight later. They brought in heavy reinforcements from Leeds, and at one stage they backed a heavy lorry into our platform, which was gallantly defended by two old friends, Jimmy Whelan from Manchester, and Norman Heys, a native of Accrington but then living in Brighouse. (I have lost touch with Jimmy, and I was sad to hear of Norman's death in September 1980).

Jimmy had recently had his teeth out and was wearing a set of dentures; as the situation grew more menacing I saw him take them out and carefully deposit them in a tin which he slipped into his pocket, ready for action. Norman grew increasingly impatient at the antics of the mob, and was muttering to me, out of the corner of his mouth: "I'll shift this lot in a minute." He could have done so, single-handed, because he was a great bull of a man who knew no fear, but I restrained him as I did not want the meeting to break up in disorder.

When we eventually closed it, we found that we were in a cul-de-sac, and that the only way out was through the mob in front of us. "What do we do now?" my friends inquired of me. There was only one answer: we go through them. We walked up to them, and I politely asked them to excuse us. This so astonished them that they obligingly parted and made way for us. We walked through them and were away before it occurred to any of them to attack us. The golden rule on such occasions is to follow the advice which Corporal Jones used to tender to Captain Mainwaring, and "don't panic." To run away would not only be cowardly, but suicidal; a steady walk is the correct procedure. Self-confidence is a valuable asset which has extracted many of us from difficult and dangerous situations.

Sheffield also provided its quota of excitement. The then secretary of the Communist Party, Harry Pollitt, addressed a meeting in Sheffield City Hall in October 1949, after a 'march' — it was more a shambling shuffle — of the comrades through the streets. A group of senior boys from a local grammar school organised a splendid counter-demonstration. They began marching behind the communists, and then broke away to take a short cut, from which they emerged in front of the reds, and led them up to the hall. The boys marched almost with the precision of the Guards, carrying Union Jacks and chanting anti-communist slogans. When the discredited communists had entered the hall for their meeting, I spoke in protest on the wide pavement outside, supported by my old Sheffield friend Frank Hamley and a few others. We were told later by our observer who had gone into the hall that Pollitt had warned his audience to be on their guard when they left the hall, as 'Fascist thugs' are mustering outside. There were in fact, I believe, seven of us and several thousands of them.

An international communist 'peace' conference was announced for Sheffield, with delegates scheduled to arrive from all over the world. We immediately announced a counter-campaign, to include a march through the city. This threw the authorities into such a panic that the march was banned, but at the same time many of the expected delegates were denied entry into Britain. This led to the cancellation of the conference, and we concluded our campaign with a victory meeting outside the City Hall. Manchester has always had a large Irish population, and I made many friends among them. The Irish are often accused of having too-long memories of past events, and this can have the effect of perpetuating old feuds and animosities. It has been truly said that "Grass grows green on the battle-field, but never on the scaffold".

But if they never forgive their enemies, the Irish never forget their friends. They still remember that it was the young Oswald Mosley who had crossed the floor of the House of Commons to protest against Black and Tan atrocities. In December 1923 the Nationalist M.P. for a Liverpool constituency and then Father of the House, T.P. O'Connor had written to Mosley's first wife, 'Cimmie' Curzon; "I regard him (Mosley) as the man who really began the break-up of the Black and Tan savagery; and I can never recall without admiration and wonder, the courage and self-sacrifice which such an attitude demanded on his part... Both your husband and yourself will always be regarded by every good Irishman with appreciation and gratitude."

This was their attitude towards me, when I advanced our policy designed to eventually end the infamous partition of Ireland, and I won much support from them, so that in February 1950 I was invited to be their guest speaker at a meeting of the Manchester Gaelic League.

Early in 1951 I broke the ban which Manchester City Council had imposed on our holding indoor meetings in the city's public halls or schools, by a simple political device. It was useless to insist that we had advanced far beyond our pre-war Fascism, to those determined to label us Fascists. So I persuaded a Conservative member of Manchester's City Council to propose a motion at a council meeting that public halls should not be let to Fascists or Communists. This created a dilemma for the communist fellow-travellers on the Labour benches in the council chamber. They did not wish to see their comrades banned from the city's halls, so they had to vote against the motion, which was consequently heavily defeated. Thereafter, for some years, we had the use of Manchester's public halls and schools, and I held our first meeting — in Claremont Road School, Moss Side — early in 1951. Our outdoor meetings continued to flourish. Door-to-door sales of Union were so successful that Manchester was usually at the top of the league table which its editor ran to encourage friendly rivalry between branches.

While stationed in Manchester I went on two speaking tours of other parts of the country. The first took me to East Anglia, where I spoke at Grantham, Spalding, Boston (at the foot of the Stump), and Lincoln. Next I toured Wessex, speaking at Portsmouth, Southampton, Poole, Winchester, Basingstoke, Newbury, Bridport, Dorchester, Weymouth, Bournemouth, Blandford Forum, and Salisbury. Among all the places at which I stayed on this tour I especially enjoyed the hospitality of a dear old friend, the late Joe Beckett, former British heavy-weight champion.

Joe had been born in a caravan on a fair-ground and had learned his boxing art the hard way, by taking on all-comers, who could earn a few shillings if they survived a round against him. They never did! He was philosophical about his defeat by the French champion Georges Carpentier, who had studied films of Joe and had noticed that he was a little slow in raising his guard at the beginning of the first round of a fight. As soon as they had touched gloves Carpentier swung a vicious hook which knocked out poor Joe, stone cold. When he came round in his dressing-room he was heard to mutter: "I was just warming up for a good fight."

His service to boxing and the prestige he had brought to Britain did not save him, or his wife, from internment under Defence Regulation 18B. He was a rough diamond in the ring, but a man of exquisite manners and quiet charm out of it. I cannot think of any original phrase with which to describe this magnificent man, so I must fall back on the old cliché: he was one of nature's gentlemen.

In 1951 I made two visits to London, to speak at a May Day rally in Ridley Road, and at a Trafalgar Square meeting in August. Between these two meetings some London members returned the compliment. Headed by their Drum Corps, a group of them marched with Manchester members from our Clowes Street bookshop to a meeting at Alexandra Park Gates.

On a Saturday evening in October of that year we heard a resounding crash, and I ran out to see a figure disappearing into the distance after having thrown a brick through our bookshop window, frightening our small son asleep upstairs. Peter survived such youthful experiences, but they may have deterred him from entering politics, although he would in those Manchester days suddenly stand up in his cot, in the middle of the night, and announce in a loud voice: "Alexandra Park Gates, 3 o'clock!" I chased our attacker, but he escaped into the darkness.

In March 1952 I came to London to speak in support of the Union Movement candidates in the local elections in Kensington, while Raven Thomson came to speak in support of my candidature in

Moss Side. Alas, in neither case was the support the movement certainly enjoyed reflected in the vote. None of us was destined to serve on a council. Old voting habits are hard to break when it comes to the point. 'Safety first' will usually prevail at the last moment. Only at times of extreme crisis, it would seem, in conditions of severe slump and mass unemployment, will any new party make much progress.

There is much that is faulty in our electoral system. Under a system of proportional representation, for instance, new and progressive parties would stand a much better chance. "Once every Preston Guild", say Lancashire folk, when their southern cousins would use some such expression as 'Once in a Blue Moon.' In fact, the 'Guild Merchant' has met in Preston every twenty years since 1542, with the exception of 1942. The Guild postponed from that year was held in the first week of September 1952. It was a wonderful experience to travel from Manchester each day, to combine Union sales and leaflet distribution with watching the colourful processions through the streets of 'Proud Preston'. This was the last of many happy events in which I took part during my years in the north-west. Before the end of the year I was recalled to London, to undertake entirely different duties, which introduced me to yet another world.

To escape the petty restrictions still being imposed on them by the authorities in England, Sir Oswald and Lady Mosley had moved to Eire, where they set up the publishing house of Euphorion Books, with a subsidiary company, Euphorion Distribution (England) Ltd., in London. These two companies published and distributed a distinguished list of books, many of them translations of classics of European literature. Among these was a new edition of Goethe's Faust, with an introduction by Oswald Mosley.

Euphorion Books achieved its one best seller in Stuka Pilot, the autobiography of the Luftwaffe ace Hans-Ulrich Rudel. Group-Captain Douglas Bader wrote a preface for the English edition,

as the French air ace Pierre Clostermann had done for the French
edition. The comradeship between these three brave men set an
example not always followed by Europe's politicians. I met Rudel
several times, this brave man who flew an incredible number
of sorties and destroyed an all-time record number of Russian
tanks, in his daring dive-bomber raids. Severely wounded, he
had had to have a leg amputated; anxious to get back into action,
he took off, his crutches beside him in his plane. He later went
to Argentina and became air adviser to Peron. I was sad to learn
of his death last December.

From their foundation the two Euphorion companies had been
run most ably by a man who now wished to move on to another
publishing house, just when the Mosleys were planning a new
and exciting venture: the launching of a literary magazine. This
project was the result of many discussions over the years as to
the best way to propagate new ideas in Britain. These discussions
had begun as far back as the pre-war days of Mosley's New
Party, whose journal *Action* had been edited by Harold Nicolson.
Nicolson was a literary rather than a political figure, and wished
to devote considerable space in the journal to reviews of books,
plays, films, etc., with a little politics, and then of a high-brow
character, tucked away on the back page.

Mosley naturally wanted more space to be given to politics: and
to 'grass-roots' politics at that. There was constant argument,
and Mosley is alleged to have said to Nicolson one day, in a
moment of exasperation: "I'm tired of people who can think; I
want people who can feel!"

The story may be apocryphal, but the British Union movement
into which the New Party developed certainly devoted most
of its time, money, and energy to courting mass support, and
showed less interest in cultivating the intelligentsia. East London
responded more vigorously to the stirring tune of the British
Union Marching Song than it would have done to the lilting
melody of Nicolson's proffered anthem, Lift High the Marigold.

The pendulum was probably swung a little too far in the direction of action; this apparent neglect of the intellectuals was a mistake which the communists never made. In the thirties they enjoyed very great success through such ventures as the Left Book Club. In fact, they succeeded in creating the impression that the words 'intellectual' and 'communist' were synonymous, and that the British Union consisted entirely of morons who could neither read nor write. A little research would have sufficed to dispose of this idea.

Some attempt to correct the imbalance had been made before the second war by means of Discussion Groups intended to supplement the *Fascist Quarterly*, a magazine which had some distinguished contributors. But it was in the immediate post-war years that the matter was seriously considered, and *The European* was launched to meet this need.

The European — subtitled The Journal of Opposition — appeared monthly from 1953 to 1959, and was a publication of great distinction. The literary standard was high. It was edited by Lady Mosley, who contributed a witty and perceptive Diary, which surveyed a wide range of topics and personalities. Over the signature European, Mosley contributed a brilliant monthly review of national and international politics and economics under the heading Analysis.

One of the purposes of *The European* was to keep Britain informed of, and in touch with, European ideas, and to counter the isolationism which had long been the British reaction to things continental. The magazine's literary contributors included Richard Aldington, Henry Williamson, Anna Cavan, Estelle Morgan, Nicholas Mosley, Roy Campbell, Peter Whigham, and Noel Stock.

Arab and Palestinian affairs were ably dealt with by Desmond Stewart, while Alan Neame introduced in translation the works of Jean Cocteau, and also contributed a brilliant commentary on

Ezra Pound's Pisan Cantos. I was shocked and grieved by the death in 1981 of Desmond Stewart, and with Alan Neame and other old friends (including John Haylock, another contributor to *The European*) attended a memorial service for him in a church near our offices. Henry Williamson, of course, was an old friend, who in 1940 had suffered arrest and a brief internment under 18B for his support of Mosley and British Union. As a boy of thirteen I had read his *Tarka the Otter* upon its publication in 1928. Although it had won the literary Hawthornden Prize, Henry hated to be reminded of it, and wished to be remembered for his novels on the first and second world wars.

Between the wars he had written his four-part *The Flax of Dream*, but he was dissatisfied with this and elaborated on its theme in his post-war *Chronicle of Ancient Sunlight*, which ran to fifteen volumes. I met Henry on many occasions, but I would not venture to say that I knew him well. Who did? He was a complex character, a man of many parts and facets. An attempt to analyse them was made in the book *Henry Williamson: The Man, The Writings*, a symposium edited by my friend Father Brocard Sewell, and published in 1980. In it friends of Henry contributed their personal impressions of him, sometimes complementary, at others almost contradictory. He remained the ex-Army officer, and young men were sometimes seen to be standing at attention while speaking to him. But it was the same Henry who is described in the book as playing leap-frog down a village street with a crowd of young people, or suggesting (in joke) that he and a fellow guest at an hotel should escape down a drain-pipe to avoid paying their bill!

Most of the literary contributors to *The European* were not members of Union Movement, however, and did not necessarily share our political opinions. Their interest in *The European* was cultural rather than political. The magazine was the only journal in the English-speaking world which kept the case of Ezra Pound consistently before the public eye until he was eventually released from the mental hospital to which the

American authorities had so shamefully committed him after the war. For this reason alone *The European* would deserve to be remembered, but in fact its bound volumes contain a wealth of fine writing and able political analysis that will ensure their being read for a long time to come.

I had never received even a day's training in journalism, printing, or publishing, so it was a formidable task to undertake the running of the Euphorion companies, in which I combined such diverse tasks as calling on bookshops and soliciting orders, invoicing, packing, despatching, keeping the books and sending out accounts, etc. For *The European* I had to edit or retype manuscripts so that they were ready for the printers, and to see them through to proof stage. At this time the Mosleys were settling down in Ireland, and each month I would take the page proofs to them in Dublin, or sometimes to Paris. I would take the night boat to Dublin, or to France, and return the following night to London, where the next morning I caught a train to Southend, where the magazine was printed, returning to London late that night. It was a strenuous but enjoyable routine.

During my days in Dublin or Paris I would go round the bookshops seeking orders for our books. I had mixed sufficiently in Irish circles to be at home with a Dublin accent, while my French was adequate to selling *The Memoirs of Alcibiades* to Parisian bookshops. On one occasion only was I baffled, when a lady buyer who had declined to place an order added something, in particularly rapid French, which sounded to my ears like: Nous achetons tous nos livres parachette. I could think of no French word like the last one in that sentence. Surely she was not telling me that they bought all their books by parachute? I continued to worry over this conundrum, and on the return boat, in mid-Channel, light broke into my darkness. Nous achetons tous nos livres par Hachette (the well known French wholesale booksellers). In this period, if I were free from work and meetings at the weekend I sometimes assisted my old friend, the late Sid Proud, in his Spanish Travel Agency. He claimed to have been the man who discovered the Costa Brava, when it was an undeveloped stretch of fishing villages. On several occasions I acted as courier for him, and each such excursion yielded some amusing or hair-raising experiences.

It would not be speaking ill of the dead to suggest that the accommodation his clients found awaiting them in Spain was not always up to the high standards promised in his lavish and luxurious brochures. We did not fly to Spain, but laboriously made our way by train and boat, leaving London on a morning train and reaching Barcelona the following evening after an exhausting journey. We would cross the frontier and enter Spain at Port Bou, where I would begin the journey southwards, on a slow local train running inland, parallel to the coast. At each stop I would hand over some of my charges to a local courier. A whispered question from each courier became a byword with us: "Do they know they're going in the annexe?"

Once I took a party to the other coast, entering Spain at Irun and taking clients on to San Sebastian, but my worst experience was having to escort two parties as far as Paris, one destined for the Costa Brava, the other for San Sebastian. The two parties totalled 197 in number, and consisted largely of dear old ladies who had never previously ventured out of England. I disembarked them safely at the Gare du Nord, whence coaches transferred them to the Gare Austerlitz. There I had to divide them into two separate parties and make sure that those catching the earlier train had their dinner before those going on a later train to the other coast. But first I had to ensure that all were present and correct.

Have you ever tried to count 197 people who refuse to stand still? I panicked mildly when a series of recounts convinced me that I was four short. Where were my dear old ladies? Locked in some French lavatory, perhaps? A wild dash back to the Gare du Nord, where I found them wandering around disconsolately, but happy to be rounded up and whisked off in a taxi. I saw little of Spain, but what I saw I loved. Europe does not end at the Pyrenees.

I contributed a good number of articles and book reviews to The European. These journalistic duties, and even more my Euphorion activities, took up so much of my time that for a few years I was forced to be much less politically active. But towards the end of 1956 things changed. I was called on at short notice to take over the organisation of two of Mosley's largest post-war meetings, one in Birmingham Town Hall, the other in Manchester's Free Trade Hall, both in October. In the same period our booking of the Adelphi Theatre, in the Strand, was cancelled by the management, so we organised a protest demonstration and sales drive outside the locked doors.

When it was over I spoke briefly from the steps of the theatre and asked our supporters to disperse quietly, but announced that I was going to walk up to Trafalgar Square to make a final protest. An enormous crowd followed, and swept me into the Square and up on to the plinth of Nelson's column, where I made a short speech, which took the police by surprise. But only for a few minutes, and then I saw two columns of the force converging on the Column.

I abruptly ended my speech, and announced: "We will now close with the National Anthem." But the police were not impressed by this patriotic gesture, and some of them climbed on to the plinth and removed me by force. I fell heavily to the ground, slightly injuring my leg, but as they had not arrested me for the offence of breaking innumerable by-laws in speaking in the Square without permission, I bore them no grudge, but made a strategic withdrawal.

In November 1955 my old friend Raven Thomson died. This left vacant the position of Secretary of Union Movement. For a year the duties of the post were carried on a temporary basis, but at Christmas 1956 Sir Oswald Mosley asked me to announce in the New Year that he had appointed me to the Secretaryship. *The European* had still another three years to run before it would cease publication, so I had to combine politics with publishing.

Chapter Thirteen

For this double role I used two names: I was Jeffrey Hamm
in politics, but became Geoffrey Vernon in publishing, to the
confusion of a number of old friends. One man in his time ...

Chapter Fourteen

They're fighting in Bramley Road", said my nine-year-old son excitedly, as he burst into the room. We had returned home (to Princedale Road, Holland Park) from our annual holiday, on the evening of the last Saturday in August, 1958. Peter had been swiftly out again to visit a corner sweet-shop, where he had heard a lady make the remark that he was now relaying to us. I walked the half-mile to Bramley Road, deep in the heart of Netting Dale, and there ran into the fiercest street fighting I had ever seen. White youths were fighting Jamaicans, and the police were struggling with both factions, to restore law and order. The North Kensington 'race riots' were in full swing.

During our holiday we had read in the newspapers of an outbreak of rioting in Nottingham the previous Saturday night, and now it had spread to London. On the following morning the Kensington organiser of Union Movement, John Wood, telephoned me to ask if I would speak for him at a meeting in the area the following evening. Objections to accepting his invitation immediately sprang to mind. I would be accused of 'stirring up race hatred', or of callously exploiting the explosive situation which already existed. On the other hand, who had a greater right than Union Movement to hold a meeting and make use of that unpopular expression: "We told you so"?

We had first drawn attention to the dangers of unrestricted coloured immigration in 1954, when we had warned of the consequences if it were not halted. At the same time we had advocated a peaceful repatriation of all post-war immigrants, then comparatively few in number, to good jobs and conditions in their homelands, to which prosperity had been restored by our economic policies. Now, sadly, we were being proved right, as we have been on so many occasions. So I accepted the invitation, and on the Monday evening I mounted a platform on the corner of Bramley Road itself. The Daily Mail estimated the audience which gathered round the platform at two thousand. I appealed for a return to law and order, and stressed that social problems can never be solved with the brick and the broken bottle, but only through the ballot-box. 'Votes, not violence!' was our slogan. The Times of 3 September reported: 'On Monday night Mr. J. Hamm, secretary of the Union Movement, held a meeting outside Latimer Road underground station. He said nothing that could be construed as an appeal to violence and limited himself to repeating that all immigration should be stopped.'

On 8 September The Times published a factual survey of the situation in North Kensington, under the banner headline: 'Union Movement not cause of racial clashes.' We were obviously entitled to campaign in the area, where I had been living for about six years at that time, and where I continued to live until 1971, on a question on which we had issued the direst warnings for the previous four years. As part of our campaign we published a local newspaper, the North Kensington Leader, copies of which were distributed free to every house in the area. This journal later devoted much space to the cases of nine local youths who were branded by the judge before whom they appeared as the cause of all the troubles in the area.

I knew the families of a number of these lads, and frequently visited their homes. North Kensington was then a rough and ready neighbourhood, in which years previously gipsy families had settled, in 'the piggeries and the potteries.' (Pottery Lane runs at the rear of Princedale Road, in which I lived). It was an area with a high crime rate, but this was confined to what the local inhabitants regarded as 'honest thieving.' If a visiting salesman was foolish enough to park his lorry and leave it unattended while he went for a drink, it was regarded by the local villains as fair game, and the goods would mysteriously fall off the back of the lorry.

But the underworld had its own code: they did not mug old women, and they did not 'grass', in the days before 'supergrasses' sold their life-stories to the national newspapers. I knew many 'villains' personally, and am never ashamed to admit that they were my friends. They did me no harm, and I could safely walk the streets of North Kensington at any hour of the day or night — something I would not dare to do now.

But the nine youths came on the whole from more 'respectable' homes, and none had any previous convictions when they stood in the dock at the Old Bailey before Mr. Justice Salmon. The learned judge had recently had before him a man who had cold-bloodedly shot his wife's lover in the stomach, killing him, and had sentenced him to three years' imprisonment. What sentence did he impose upon the nine youths? Four years each, an infamous sentence against which we campaigned relentlessly, but without success.

We opened a Union Movement bookshop in Kensington Park Road, where I conducted a weekly political 'surgery', to which the local people flocked with their varied problems. Many of these concerned housing in an area where people lived, ate, and slept — six or seven adults and children — in one room. Will anyone say that we were not entitled to draw attention to such conditions ?

We never suggested that immigration had caused the housing shortage — an absurd notion — but we attacked the no less absurd policy of encouraging unrestricted immigration into such an area, thereby grossly aggravating the already existing basic problem. I kept a 'case book', and was able to record at least some success in each of over fifty cases that I handled at this time. Some of them were spectacular: the rehousing of one family, the clearing of foul-smelling decaying rubbish from a basement area adjacent to a room in which a young baby slept. The local Medical Officer of Health complained that I should not regard his office as 'a panacea for all ills', but he sprang into much-delayed action when I telephoned him to say that I was on my way to the spot with a press photographer. We put the telephone down and raced there, but a council lorry and an emergency squad of workmen beat us to it, and were shovelling away like men possessed when we entered the street.

A lady complained to me that her coloured landlord had the habit of coming upstairs on a Sunday morning to collect her rent with rent-book in one hand and a knife in the other, in an effort to persuade her to leave so that he could re-let her flat at some exorbitant rent. I informed the local police, who declined to act, insisting that this was a domestic 'landlord and tenant' dispute, and that the correct procedure was for her to apply to the magistrates for a summons against the landlord. She did so, and a date was fixed for the hearing: some six months ahead.

She was genuinely in fear that by that time her throat would have been cut, so some more dramatic action seemed to be indicated. I telephoned the police again and informed them that the lady had invited me to her flat for a cup of tea at 10a.m. on the following Sunday; the time the landlord called for his rent. The police warned me to stay away, and threatened me with arrest if there were any breach of the peace! I told them that I had no intention of causing any breach of the peace, but every intention of accepting the invitation I had received. As I walked into the street on the Sunday morning I was confronted with a massive police patrol — police cars, motorcycles, constables on foot. I rang the bell, was admitted, enjoyed my cup of tea — and emerged unscathed. The landlord never threatened the lady again.

Another interesting case was that of Mrs. Warren, of Bletchingdon Street. Her coloured landlord applied for an eviction order against her, on the grounds that he required the house where she had lived all her life for his family, who were coming from the West Indies to join him in London. The local Citizens' Advice Bureau arranged for her to be represented at Willesden County Court, on Legal Aid. The landlord was granted his eviction order, and the poor lady was then presented with a bill from the Law Society for £80: her contribution to the costs after an 'assessment' of her income. After an exchange of letters with the Law Society I succeeded in getting the demand reduced to £30. They sued her for that amount, and the case was heard at Clerkenwell County Court, where Mrs. Warren asked me to appear for her. I explained to her that I was neither a solicitor nor a barrister, and therefore had no right to be heard, but that if she called me as a witness I would say as much as I could before the judge ruled me out of order and told me to leave the box.

The ruse worked, and I was able to put before the judge much of Mrs. Warren's grievances before he peered at me over his spectacles and asked: "Are you some sort of solicitor?" I was not sure what 'some sort of solicitor' might be, but I pleaded not guilty. Counsel for the Law Society had put my letters to the Society before the court; in one of them I had stated that we would be prepared to have Mrs. Warren represented, if the matter were pursued. He scornfully commented: "She is here today, and is not represented!"

I seized the opportunity to explain to the judge that we had offered to provide representation, but that the poor lady had become so distressed by this time that she had said she did not wish it. The judge accepted this explanation and he was extremely sympathetic to Mrs. Warren. He anxiously inquired whether she could not seek the assistance of her Member of Parliament. I replied that she had no faith in that gentleman; that was why she had turned to me. "Could she not apply for legal aid?", he innocently mused, and then hastily corrected himself: "Good God, no! That is the last thing the poor woman would want!"

As the Law Society had proved that counsel had legitimately been paid the amount demanded the judge had no option but to give judgement in its favour. He reluctantly made an order for her to pay in small weekly instalments, with no order for costs, which we thought was a moral victory for us.

No visitor to our 'surgery' ever charged us with doing nothing for them; in cases where we secured only very minor results they were grateful to us for at least trying, where the old political parties had ignored them.

In North Kensington there was now much popular clamour for Mosley to contest the constituency at the next election, as a true people's champion. His acceptance of the invitation produced one of the most extraordinary adoption meetings of all time. It was held in the Argyll Hall, North Kensington, on 6 April 1959. Three local newspapers reported the meeting. The Kensington News said that 'Thunderous applause, cheering, and foot-stamping greeted Sir Oswald Mosley as he stepped on to the platform.' According to the Kensington Post 'A cheering, stamping audience packed the Argyll Hall to hear Sir Oswald Mosley.' When a member of the audience asked Mosley why he was standing in North Kensington, the paper reported that the audience shouted its own reply: "Because we want him !"

Football fans will know that Shepherds Bush is the home of Queens Park Rangers, and will appreciate John Brunei of the Shepherds Bush Gazette writing of 'an audience brought to the frenzy of a cup-tie crowd by brilliant political oratory. At the conclusion of each and every point a cheer went up louder than a Loftus Road roar when the Rangers have scored. Hats were thrown into the air. People stamped their feet in applause. A few men even stood on their chairs and jumped for joy.'

The campaign continued on this high note up to the election period, when the pace became intense. Mosley spoke at four street-corner meetings every evening for several weeks before polling day, 8 October. I had to work to a tight schedule. I would open the first meeting, and then hand over the platform to Mosley on his arrival. Then I would be driven to the site of the second meeting, and then on to the third and fourth, adopting the same procedure at each. We canvassed assiduously, and the campaign culminated in the greatest eve-of-poll meeting I have ever witnessed.

Mosley spoke from a loudspeaker van parked in a street in the Golborne area, the most northerly part of the constituency. At the end of the meeting he walked back to our committee rooms, followed by a surging and cheering crowd which blocked the wide main thoroughfare, road and pavements, wall to wall. As a result of our canvass we thought we 'knew our vote'. The task on polling day is to 'poll your vote.'

On polling day our team worked hard, without letting up. We were helped by additional volunteers in the evening, checking poll-cards, marking up our canvass-sheets, 'knocking up' stragglers who had not yet voted. As soon as the poll closed a vast cavalcade of cars, vans, lorries, motor-cycles, with horns blaring and headlights blazing, swept from North Kensington down to the Town Hall, in Kensington High Street, where the result was to be declared. To say that the result stunned us would be the understatement of all time. Mosley was credited with 2,821 votes out of a total of almost 35,000, and was bottom of the poll. Not only were all our women supporters in tears, but many of the men too wept unashamedly, shocked and stunned by this anti-climax.

After a sleepless night I went to the committee rooms the following morning to perform that most doleful of all last rites: the sweeping up of torn election addresses, leaflets, posters, which had now become waste paper. Some of us had experienced too many elections to remain deflated for long, and not one of us questioned the validity of the result. But then local people began to call on us, to express their disbelief. How could this be? they asked. With some exaggeration, some of them insisted that from their street alone more than two thousand people had voted for Mosley. Could there possibly be some mistake? Had there been some error, accidental or intentional?

We began to review all we had seen and heard during the campaign, and to pose to ourselves questions which have never been satisfactorily answered. It had been a high-powered campaign, with the old parties bringing up their big guns against our by no means insignificant machine. The press of the world had been present, supported by radio and television, until the whole constituency buzzed with excitement. Was it not odd, therefore, that the total poll was low, well beneath the national average?

Our canvass had been conducted by men and women of long experience, not easily hoodwinked by the busy housewife prepared to promise her vote to any canvasser who will leave her in peace. Could they all have been mistaken? We scarcely ever encountered hostility to Mosley, who had been nursing the constituency for a long time before the election, and had become a familiar and popular figure in the locality. Towards the Labour candidate, the sitting member George Rogers, there was considerable hostility, because of his alleged laziness and indifference in dealing with complaints and grievances.

On all sides we heard the opinion expressed that if Mosley should fail to win, victory would go to the strongly-fancied popular Conservative candidate Bob Bulbrook, leaving Rogers a rank outsider. The local bookmakers, those experts who become rich by developing a keen nose for the winner and the outsider, were offering only even money on Bulbrook and Mosley. Yet Rogers won, if only by the narrow majority of 877 votes. Could the bookies have all been wrong too?

We decided to investigate the possibility that there had been some gigantic swindle, and I played some part in organising and conducting our inquiry. We began from the fact of the low poll. Armed with certified copies of the election registers which had been used in the polling stations we called on some of those whose names had not been crossed off, i.e. electors shown as not having voted. As far as possible we used new canvassers, who did not necessarily reveal their identity, but simply said they were inquiring into the reasons for the low poll. "Why did you not vote?" we would ask on the doorstep. "But I did", came the reply, over and over again. In a short time we had collected one hundred names of people adamant that they had voted, but whose names were not crossed off on the registers. We could undoubtedly have gathered many more had we continued.

We then called again on these one hundred electors, accompanied by a Commissioner for Oaths, and invited them to swear affidavits as to the time and place where they had voted, with a view to challenging the validity of the election in the High Court. Unfortunately, the word 'court' has always had a remarkable effect on the good people of North Kensington, with its high proportion of inhabitants with considerable experience of courts, and of the prisons to which they sometimes led — as the result perhaps of unfortunate deals in commodities which persistently fell from the backs of lorries. On our second visit an extraordinary amnesia seemed to have set in. People could not now remember whether they had voted or not. They had intended voting, but perhaps on second thoughts they had not. Our original one hundred were whittled down to twenty, but these stood fast and signed their affidavits.

On 29 October 1959 Sir Oswald Mosley presented a petition to the High Court, asking for the result of the election in North Kensington to be declared invalid, because of a number of irregularities, contrary to the Representation of the People Acts. The hearing of the case opened before Mr. Justice Streatfield and Mr. Justice Slade on 4 April 1960, and continued for three days. Mosley appeared in person; the Returning Officer and others concerned were represented by counsel. It was a fascinating experience for me to have been of some assistance in preparing the case, and to sit beside Mosley in court, by which time I had all the complicated documents at my finger-tips.

But what happened before the hearing? We had called on our twenty witnesses to serve on them witness summonses and to hand each of them a £1 'conduct fee'; and here we encountered some strange experiences. People who had hitherto been extremely friendly now refused to open their doors to us, and in some cases were literally cowering behind the curtains at their windows. Some opened their doors, but refused to accept the £1 and sign the witness summons. What had happened? Who had approached them and terrified them in this way? These questions will never now be answered. Of the twenty witnesses subpoenaed ten failed to attend court, and of the ten who gave evidence five now insisted that they had not voted!

There are elaborate rules for the conduct of elections, set out in minute detail in the Representation of the People Acts and their schedules. A serious breach of them may constitute an 'illegal practice' and render the offender liable to prosecution. It was conceded that in this election there had been some breaches of the rules, but they did not constitute an illegal practice. Did they render the election invalid? No, because it had been 'conducted substantially in accordance with the law' and 'the result was not materially affected'. Apparently the result would have been 'materially affected' only if we had been able to present 878 breaches of the rules: one more than the Labour candidate's majority!

The petition was therefore dismissed by Mr. Justice Streatfield. Mr. Justice Slade, concurring, added that he wished to 'acknowledge the courtesy, ability, and clarity with which Sir Oswald has argued his case'. The fifties ended, and the sixties opened, with my receiving an increasing number of invitations to speak at universities, in Wales, Scotland and Ireland, as well as in many parts of England. In February 1959 I paid the first of several visits to St. David's College, Lampeter, now part of the University of Wales, and in October 1960 I was at St. Andrew's University, in Scotland. These were enjoyable occasions, with serious debate far into the night, and resumed the following morning over coffee. In February 1961 I took part in debates at Nottingham and Bangor universities, and in May I visited Swansea.

Each of these three engagements produced a mildly amusing incident. At Nottingham the speeches from the floor were so strongly in favour of the motion I had proposed that I had to pinch myself to make sure that I was not dreaming of my first victory in a university debate. But the dream turned sour when the vote was taken. Hundreds of students who had not attended the debate were allowed to flock into the chamber and vote, to ensure my overwhelming defeat.

Bangor had a girl President of Debates that year, and I had written to her to say that I must be back in London in the morning after the debate, as I had an important engagement. She told me that if the debate dragged on and I missed the last train from Bangor, she would drive me across Anglesey to Holyhead, where I could catch the Irish mail train to Euston, which did not stop at Bangor. The President allowed the debate to get completely out of hand, and speakers were hurling insults at me, with no possible relevance to the motion.

I sat impassively through these tirades, but kept looking at the clock to see if there was still a chance that I might catch the last train. But to have left abruptly would have looked as if I were running away, and would have deprived me of the opportunity of making a brief reply, to put the record straight. So I stayed, and replied with a few carefully chosen words which reduced my opponents to howling and whistling. The debate ended, and the President, now full of sweetness and light, offered me coffee before driving me to Holyhead.

I declined, and forgot the golden rule that a gentleman should never be rude to a lady, as I added a few more well chosen words. Then I walked out, through the howling and hissing mob, vowing that I would hitch a lift from Bangor to London, or walk the whole way — as Baron Corvo once did from Holywell to London — rather than accept a lift from Madam President.

As I was hurrying down the hill to the station, hoping that the train might be running late, I heard footsteps behind me, and turned ready to defend myself. But instead of an attack a young man, breathless from running, blurted out his apologies for the way I had been treated, and assured me that the mob represented only a minority of the students: an assurance that I gladly accepted. The London train was late, and I caught it with time to spare.

At Swansea I spoke during the students' lunch hour, and was asked to return in the evening to address the Faculty of Political Science. This sounded like a challenging invitation. After an afternoon exploring the city and its magnificent bay I faced the economic experts, headed by their lecturer. I challenged their orthodoxies with our post-Keynesian heresies until their lecturer could stand it no longer. He stormed out, intending to slam the door behind him, but he was frustrated as it was one of those weighted doors that can close only slowly and quietly.

During 1960 and 1961 the Labour Party and its allies ran a mounting campaign for the boycott of South African goods. We opposed the campaign, just as we had resisted a similar attack on trade with pre-war Germany, because the sparks of a trade dispute can easily ignite the forest fires of war. When the Labour Party threatened to picket shops selling South African goods we announced that we would counter-picket, and urge potential customers to enter the shops and buy South African products. The proposed Labour Party pickets did not relish the prospect of a confrontation, and called off that part of the campaign.

We sold Action at a Labour Party meeting in Trafalgar Square. Mosley came to encourage us, and afterwards he led an informal march of our sellers back to our offices. Subsequent trade figures revealed that trade with South Africa had actually soared during the time of the attempted boycott.

In March 1962 Mosley convened a conference in Venice of Europeans from a number of countries, and a Declaration of Venice was issued, stating a common policy on which all could come together in forming a 'National Party of Europe.' Unfortunately, much of the enthusiasm manifested at the conference evaporated when the delegates got home and faced criticism that a concrete project of this kind was too precipitate, and consequently Mosley's idea never got off the ground. The beating of the nationalist drum is no doubt exciting for those content to march up the hill and down again bearing a banner with a strange device and shouting meaningless slogans. But the derisory and falling votes polled by nationalist candidates in the elections of February and October 1974, and again in May 1979, prove that nationalism does not win elections.

I was unable to attend the Venice Conference as I was engaged in my first Parliamentary election, a by-election in Middlesborough. My agent went to Venice, while his candidate languished in Middlesborough, during a particularly severe winter. I managed to get together a small team which gave what time it could to canvassing, but most days I tramped the snow-bound streets alone, knocking on doors when I could reach them through the snowdrifts, shouting through a loud-hailer when people indoors wisely refused to open them to me or to the wintry blasts. I polled badly, but this daunting experience in no way diminished my affection for the warm-hearted people of the northeast.

The year 1962 saw a revival of highly organised communist violence directed against our meetings, linked to a vicious Press campaign. Mosley spoke in Trafalgar Square on 13 May, and was widely advertised to speak there again on 22 July. A few weeks before that latter day, Colin Jordan of his so-called 'British Movement' spoke at a lunatic fringe meeting in the Square. This gave the Reds a pretext for whipping up feeling against Mosley.

I was in the Square early on the afternoon of our meeting, and I saw serried ranks of communists standing silently behind an obviously inadequate police cordon, a single thin blue line. The meeting was due to begin at 3p.m., and I stood at the foot of Nelson's column, watching the hands of the clock on the church of St. Martin-in-the-

Field move towards the hour. As the clock struck three I climbed on to the plinth and walked to the microphone. Suddenly a single figure appeared in front of the plinth. Putting his hands on it, he tried to hoist himself up, and his face appeared in front of me. He presented a beautiful sitting target, and I gave him a straight right which knocked him to the ground.

At that moment hundreds of screaming communists seemed to arrive from all points of the compass. (My would-be assailant had either jumped the gun, or had run faster than the others). Our slogan-boards along the plinth were smashed, and the pieces tossed into the air. After a few minutes of fierce fighting the police managed to restore order, but they ordered the meeting to close, before Mosley had even arrived.

This abortive meeting gave us at least one fine new member, who has remained loyal to us ever since. Harry was at that time a young man not particularly interested in politics, and happened to be taking a Sunday afternoon stroll around Trafalgar Square. There he was astonished to see a group of communists being issued with tins which had contained food for the pigeons, and with old pennies. They were being instructed by their leader to squash the tins flat so that they had sharp and jagged edges, and to sharpen the pennies to rims as thin as razor blades. What were they to do with the tins and the pennies? Their leader was specific: he pointed at me as I was walking towards the microphone, and gave his instructions: "Aim for his eyes!"

Harry turned away in disgust, pushed his way to the plinth, and joined us on the spot. The violence continued. At a Ridley Road meeting on 31 July Mosley's life was put in jeopardy, when he was set upon by a gang of communist thugs, and brought to the ground. Mosley saved himself from serious injury by holding one of his attackers on top of him, while his son Max was quickly to his rescue. On this occasion Mosley would have been killed, or at least gravely injured, but for his own strength and presence of mind, and the quick intervention of his son.

A little before the Ridley Road attack on Mosley, some of us had travelled to Manchester to join Northern members in a march from an assembly point near Bellevue. Fighting broke out even before we had moved off, and the march was subjected to constant attack and a heavy barrage of missiles from a highly organised communist opposition. We reached the site of our meeting, and Mosley mounted a loudspeaker van and began to speak. After about fifteen minutes the police asked him to close the meeting, as it was becoming increasingly difficult to hold back the mob. As always, he obeyed the law, closing the meeting and driving off, taking with him women members and others who might easily be injured in a fight. I stayed behind to ensure that our remaining members were safe, and I spoke to the then Chief Constable of Manchester, Sir John McKay, whom I had known when he had been stationed in London, and later in Birmingham. I told him that I was familiar with Manchester, and that I would direct our small band to the nearest bus stop and see them out of the troubled area. He approved, and I left him. Sporadic fighting continued, but we moved steadily towards our bus stop.

Then occurred one of those ludicrous incidents which often reduce a serious situation to farce. I have for many years enjoyed the most friendly relations with the police, and I have a particularly high regard for the police of Manchester. But there is an exception to every rule, and an eccentric character in every fine body of men. On this occasion it was an officious constable who quite unnecessarily started pushing our people in the back, and shouting to them to hurry along. I remonstrated with him, and he retaliated by arresting me.

I was taken to the nearest police station, but not to the charge-room or to a cell. Instead, I was entertained with cups of tea in the canteen, where exhausted police officers were reviving themselves after their strenuous labours. One was telephoning to his wife: "I'll be late home, luv. There's been a bit of a punch-up." This was a mild euphemism for a battle which had ended with forty-seven arrests, forty-four of those arrested being our opponents.

An officer came into the canteen and asked me why I had been arrested. I explained that I had committed no offence, and I knew no more about the matter than he did. He left me under the impression that he was going to order my release, but perhaps it was considered that the wheels of justice, once set in motion, must continue to roll. I was called from the canteen not to the station exit but to the charge-room, where the charge was read out with great solemnity. I was accused of 'obstructing the free passage of the highway, contrary to Section 1 of the Highways Act, 1959'. I was then released on bail, and stayed in Manchester overnight, to appear in court the following morning.

In court, as I was waiting for my name to be called, I watched with some cynicism communists being fined paltry sums for such serious offences as carrying offensive weapons. As each stepped from the dock a prominent Manchester business man wrote out a cheque for the fine and handed it to the gaoler. British justice is indeed 'the best that money can buy'. When my turn came, I interrupted this smooth course of events by pleading not guilty. I was then remanded on bail, to appear the following week. It would, of course, have been much simpler and less expensive to have pleaded guilty, but I had a strong objection to this, since I was entirely innocent of any offence.

At the resumed hearing the officer who had arrested me told the magistrates that he had asked me to move on after the meeting, and that I had moved 'about a yard' and then stopped. He had again asked me to move, and I had moved 'about another yard'. At a third request from him I had 'stood with both feet firmly planted on the ground', so he had arrested me.

This somewhat colourful evidence he further embroidered by adding that I had been 'surrounded by a hostile crowd of eighty or ninety people'. At the conclusion of his evidence the Clerk of the Court put to me the routine inquiry: did I wish to ask the officer any questions? The response is almost invariably no, or else just one or two halting questions. The courts do not encourage lengthy cross-examinations, and when I embarked on one the Clerk constantly interrupted me. To such conduct there is a simple remedy: I suggested to the magistrates that if their learned Clerk was determined to interrupt my cross-examination it might save everyone's time if they convicted me without further ado, and then I could take the matter to a higher court. This had the desired effect of silencing the Clerk.

The police officer's evidence had provided material for a little gentle teasing. Had there really been eighty or ninety hostile people around me? If so, would they not have been causing a greater obstruction of the highway than I was, and should they not all have been arrested? Perhaps he had not arrested them because it was easier to arrest me? He agreed. What was the significance of his evidence that I had been standing 'with both feet planted firmly on the ground'? Was it seriously suggested that I should have stood on my head and waved my feet in the air? By this time the magistrates were laughing, but the show must go on. They pretended to be in such grave doubt that it would be necessary for them to retire to their room to consider their decision. We stood and bowed, and off they trooped. A few minutes later they returned, and we stood and bowed again. "There is an element of doubt in this case, and the defendant must be given the benefit of it. The case is dismissed." Such was the verdict handed down from the Delphic oracle. I applied for costs, to cover my train fares between London and Manchester, but these were refused as the case 'had been quite properly brought.' The Press whisked me off to a nearby pub, where over much beer they tried to incite me to bring an action for unlawful imprisonment, but I declined, as I wished my friendly relationship with the Manchester police to continue.

My next appearance in court was in a very different capacity. I had come across an obscure Act of Parliament, passed to counter the disturbances created by militant suffragettes at political meetings in the early years of this century. This was the Public Meetings Act of 1908, a short single-sheet Act which lays it down that 'it shall be deemed an offence at a lawful public meeting to behave in a disorderly manner for the purpose of preventing the transaction of the business for which the meeting was called together.'

The Act required the Chairman of the meeting to take out a summons against the offender, but this had proved impracticable, as the names and addresses of such offenders were not normally known, and they could not be compelled to disclose them.

This anomaly was not corrected until the passing of the Public Order Act of 1936, which empowered a police officer to demand a name and address if requested to do so by the Chairman of a public meeting, and if he were satisfied that an offence had been committed under the 1908 Act.

One day when I was Chairman of a street meeting in Croydon I told the police inspector on duty that I proposed adopting this procedure. I watched a man in the crowd persistently interrupting the speaker, and I asked for his name and address to be taken. Armed with this information I went the following morning to Croydon Magistrates Court to apply for a summons.

A magistrate decided to hear my application in his private room. He was reluctant to grant it, and argued that the man was 'only heckling', something one should expect at a political meeting. I replied that there was nothing in law to say that 'only heckling' was legal, but that in any case this had not been ordinary heckling, but a systematic attempt to disrupt the meeting.

I added that I very much doubted whether the Annual General Meeting of the Magistrates' Association was conducted to an accompaniment of shouting, booing, and singing, so why should a lawful public meeting of an established political organisation be subject to different rules?

He grudgingly granted my application, and a summons was served on Dean Raffaele Sargeant, a member of the Yellow Star organisation. I presented my case against him at the Croydon court on 5 November 1962. My evidence was corroborated by the police inspector, and Dean Raffaele Sargeant, who had been represented by counsel, was convicted. The penalty was only a conditional discharge, but a principle had been established. At a later date I successfully used the same procedure at a meeting in Bethnal Green, taking out summonses at Old Street Magistrates' Court, and securing the conviction of three men, who were fined.

We had survived the resurrection of organised violence, and I felt that my enforcement of the law through these court actions had made some small contribution to law and order. Those of us who believe, rightly or wrongly, that we advance positive policies and constructive solutions to Britain's problems have nothing to fear from the free expression of all opinions. It is those who have no real policies of their own, and no effective reply to ours, who seek refuge in 'punch-up politics'.

Chapter Fifteen

The year 1963 opened with a visit to South Wales in February. I had been in correspondence with the secretary of a South Wales church group, the Barry Island United Men's Fellowship, and with the President of Debates at St. David's College, Lampeter, where I had previously spoken, to arrange consecutive dates for me to speak to them.

My plans were announced in the South Wales Echo, which reported 'a spontaneous protest' against my visit to Barry. But it appeared to be organised rather than spontaneous; the report said that protests had come from 'trade unionists, Muslims, and Jews', an improbable alliance, and one not likely to be encountered in a Welsh pub on Saturday night.

As I stepped off the train at Cardiff reporters and television men were waiting for me on the platform, and I was filmed walking to the barrier. My arrival was announced on the next TV news bulletin, and the film was shown on the following day, in the afternoon Welsh bulletin, and later in the evening news in English.

Under pressure from the 'spontaneous' protesters, the Barry secretary had cancelled my engagement. I stayed with friends in Bridgend overnight, and travelled on to Lampeter the next day, accompanied by a television crew. The Western Mail reported that a petition asking the authorities to ban my appearance at the Debating Society had been 'taken down from the college notice board at the weekend after only two signatures had been written on the sheet of paper. It had been on display for three days.' The report continued: "The 200 students at the college are generally in favour of hearing about the movement.'

This was confirmed the following day when the Western Mail recorded that 'two-thirds of the total number of students in the college turned out for the meeting', in a snow blizzard. Question time was described as having been 'heated'; this might not have been disagreeable under the weather conditions, but in fact I received an uninterrupted hearing, and loud applause at the end of my speech. The entire proceedings were filmed, and extracts shown twice the following day, both in Welsh and English television news bulletins.

The organised communist violence of 1962 had been made an excuse for banning further Union Movement meetings in Trafalgar Square, in spite of the fact that in the previous four years we had held seven large and enthusiastic rallies there with no, or only negligible, disorder. Yet the Press, whose duty it is to report events objectively, created and perpetuated the myth that in 1962 Mosley had suddenly emerged from retirement or exile, and that his reappearance had 'naturally' provoked 'a spontaneous uprising' against him.

For seven years we had had a meeting in Trafalgar Square on the second Sunday in May, but in 1963 our application for use of the Square was refused by the Government, as was every subsequent application. Following the example of the Government, practically every local authority reverted to refusing us the use of municipal halls, so we had to think of new methods of propaganda. We informed the police that we intended holding a sales drive for our journal *Action* in and around Trafalgar Square, but the Government banned this too. The ban was issued on the day, 12 May, when a gang of thugs — later identified as belonging to the Yellow Star organisation - broke into our offices and brutally assaulted my colleague Robert Row, the editor of *Action,* and another colleague.

They bound Robert Row hand and foot, and then repeatedly kicked him in the face and all over his body. Six men eventually pleaded guilty at the Old Bailey to this dastardly and cowardly assault, and to malicious damage, and were fined staggering sums — ranging from £10 to £35!

An exceptionally interesting debate was held at Queen's University, Belfast, in February 1965. I had visited Dublin on a number of occasions, but this was my first visit to 'Black North', and my first impressions were not favourable. The coach from the airport skirted the Falls Road area, scene of so much violence and tragedy a few years later, but the warmth of my reception at the university soon made up for the bleakness of my journey.

My opponent in debate was the late Robert Pitman, at that time a columnist and book reviewer on the *Daily Express* and *Sunday Express*, and he was accompanied by his charming wife Pat. Robert died tragically at an early age, and his widow later married the journalist, author, and historian Colin Cross, who spoke at an Action dinner in December 1978.

It was a great pleasure to meet Pat again on that occasion, and she later kindly sent me a copy of *An Encyclopaedia of Crime,* which she had written in collaboration with Colin Wilson. Having no copies left of the English edition, she offered me one in Chinese, but that is not one of my languages, so I settled for a copy of the Spanish edition.

In the Belfast debate I had been asked to propose the motion: 'This House believes that Britain's first loyalty should be to Europe, not to the Commonwealth.' Robert Pitman, as a *Daily Express* man, was a disciple of Lord Beaverbrook, and I remember indulging in a little gentle teasing about his 'Imperial' policies, which seemed to us quite obsolete in a post-Imperial world, and saying something to this effect: "*The Daily Express* office in Fleet Street is constructed almost entirely of glass, but for some reason which modern science cannot explain no light penetrates therein" .

So Mr. Pitman and his colleagues sit in utter darkness, chained like Empire Crusaders, crying, with Goethe: "Mehr licht!" During the debate there was much coming and going, with students disappearing through the swing doors at the rear of the great hall, and returning a little later. It was some time before I realised that they were making for the bar, no doubt to stimulate their faculties for debate. This became clear when a great bearded giant lurched out into the central aisle and bellowed: "Mr. President, sir. On a point of information, are ye aware that certain members of this House are drunk?" But the standard of debate rose rather than fell with the lateness of the hour and the consumption of beer, and some of the best speeches were made after midnight.

I was delighted when I won this debate. Afterwards the Pitmans and I were driven some miles out of the city to a village pub with which the students, so they informed us, had 'a sort of arrangement', to which the licensing laws did not seem to apply. When we arrived there in the early hours of the morning the place was packed, and I enjoyed generous student hospitality until it was time for breakfast and my return flight to London.

At the first General Election after the Second World War the late Sir Edward Boyle had been elected Conservative member of Parliament for the Handsworth division of Birmingham. Handsworth was at that time a most agreeable suburb, and the good Tory ladies of Handsworth Wood were thrilled at having 'Dear Sir Edward', as their member. But doubts arose when he declared himself totally opposed to any restrictions on immigration, already a problem in neighbouring constituencies.

His majority declined steadily with successive elections, and by mid-1965 staunch Tories were insisting that never again would they campaign for Edward Boyle, or even give him their vote. A friend invited me to Birmingham, where I met privately some of these dissident Tories, who invited me to contest the constituency, with their support. I was officially adopted as their prospective Union Movement candidate at a meeting held in Handsworth on Sunday, 31 October 1965.

We knew that a General Election could not be long delayed, and we began work at once. Apart from a short Christmas break I travelled to Birmingham every weekend up to the election period six months later. Every Sunday afternoon I led a team of workers who distributed at least one piece of propaganda literature to every single house and flat in the large and straggling constituency, while we managed to deliver a second piece to about half the area. We had no difficulty in getting my nomination papers completed, and they carried the signatures of former well known Handsworth Conservatives prepared to declare their new allegiance openly in this way.

My adoption was reported in the *Birmingham Post* and *Birmingham Mail,* but thereafter I was asked by the editor of the *Birmingham Planet* if I would give his paper information in advance of his rivals, and I agreed to do so. The Planet was a tabloid, owned by Mr. Woodrow Wyatt, and the editor and one of his reporters honoured their side of the bargain by giving my advance campaign considerable publicity. Then came nomination day, and at this point *The Planet* abruptly changed its tactics. It reported the nomination of two candidates, Sir Edward Boyle (Conservative) and Mrs. Sheila Wright (Labour), but it made no mention of the third candidate, myself. In following issues the Planet spoke of the 'straight fight' between Sir Edward Boyle and Mrs. Wright; again no mention of me. Whenever I telephoned to the Planet office to complain, the editor and the reporter were always mysteriously out or engaged. This farce was kept up until the election.

At the previous election there had been a very able Liberal candidate in Handsworth, Mr. Wallace Lawlor, Birmingham's first Liberal councillor. To my relief, he decided to move to the neighbouring Ladywood constituency, where he was elected, only to die suddenly, while still a young man. He had campaigned vigorously on the housing conditions in the poorer part of Handsworth, bordering on the Aston Villa football ground. As soon as it was announced that he would not be contesting Handsworth I switched much of my campaigning to that area, where I was given the same friendly reception that I had received in Handsworth Wood.

My band of willing helpers were running a sweepstake on how many votes I would obtain. They were all suffering acutely from that dangerous disease known as 'election fever', whose chief symptom is a conviction that victory is in sight because some good lady had smiled at your canvasser on her doorstep. My own estimate would have been much more cautious than theirs; but I did not want to dampen their enthusiasm, so I declined to join in their sweepstake.

We fought a hard but clean campaign, and entered the Town Hall for the count. Sir Edward Boyle accidentally bumped against me, and apologised with excessive politeness. Mrs. Sheila Wright was overheard to comment on 'all those votes going to Hamm'. How many? A highly satisfactory figure of 1,337, or 4.1 per cent of the total votes recorded, some 20,000 of the 51,000 electors on the register having abstained from voting.

Why did I regard this vote as 'highly satisfactory'? I had anticipated that a lot of my Tory supporters in the end would take fright at the possibility of Mrs. Wright winning the seat if they voted for me. Their last-minute reaction would be: "Better vote for old Boyle again, I suppose. Don't want to let that awful Labour woman in!" I knew that I was likely to fall between two stools, and also that I would probably suffer from the apathy of abstainers.

The election over, I complained to the Press Council about the behaviour of the *Birmingham Planet*. In its defence the Planet pleaded that "an error was made through oversight by the writer of the article in the issue of March 24", and that they had published a correction on "one of the main news pages ... set in bold type" — on polling day! The Press Council's adjudication read: 'The Birmingham Planet failed in its duty to the electors of the constituency by omitting from its issue of 17 and 24 March 1966 the name of a candidate who had been validly nominated, while publishing the names of the two other candidates. The complaint is upheld.'

In 1966 Oswald Mosley began to write his autobiography, *My Life*, or rather to dictate it on to cassettes, which he would post to me from his home in France. Cassettes and typed transcripts, which always needed revision and a retyping, shuttled to and fro between France and England at a furious pace, as the book began to take shape. It was in this period that he made the momentous decision to 'withdraw from party warfare'.

That was the exact formula he employed, and it meant exactly what it said, no more, no less. It did not mean that he had retired from politics. In fact, he was more active in the years following that announcement, and the publication of his autobiography in 1968, than in any previous phase of his life. But the form of his activity was different. He had reverted to one of his earliest ideas: that government by one party alone can never be efficient.

He had discovered this almost at the time he entered Parliament, at the age of twenty-two, in 1918. He would often relate how, after a heated debate in the House of Commons, he would be invited to dinner at a friend's house, and would find himself sitting next to an opponent of the afternoon or earlier evening. Many leading politicians would express regret on such private occasions that 'they were always fighting each other', when they 'ought to be on the same side'. The concept of a 'Centre Party' was much discussed in those parliamentary circles, long before the New Party was launched by Mosley after his resignation from the second Labour Government, in which he had been a Minister.

That resignation has been much criticised, by Mosley's friends as well as his foes, who unite in agreeing that if he had remained in Parliament he would have become either a Labour or a Conservative Prime Minister. But he was right to resign, because it was impossible to carry through the necessary radical reforms with the antiquated machinery of the Labour Party. His New Party failed because of the confidence trick of the so-called 'National' Government which swept to power in 1931.

The whole course of history might have been changed if three men had been consulted in the formation of a real National Government in that year. Humphry Berkeley defined them as "a former Prime Minister, a future Prime Minister, and the only man of whom it has been said that he might have been either a Labour or Conservative Prime Minister". They were, of course, Lloyd George, Winston Churchill, and Oswald Mosley.

Lloyd George had been seriously ill and was recuperating abroad when a National Government was being discussed. Winston Churchill was so far outside the pale, as far as the Tory Establishment was concerned (before the war years in which he became its tribal deity) that Lady Churchill was to write: "My husband was more hated than Mosley ever was." Mosley himself, 'the young man in a hurry', had burned his boats by launching his New Party. So government was entrusted to 'a Ministry of all the muttons', which muddled us in 1939 into that disastrous war which cost 50,000,000 lives, lost us the British Empire, and enslaved half Europe and half Asia under communism.

Surely the record of all the old political parties to date suggests that Britain's problems can never be solved by any one of them. So why should a coalition of them be any more successful? Why should a coalition of the parties of failure under the SDP label or any other, produce success? In Mosley's aphorism: Zero plus zero will always equal zero.

Mosley 'withdrew from party warfare' in 1966 and became once more what he had described himself as being in *The Alternative* (1947): 'A man without a party'. From that position, outside and above party politics, he continued to advocate, up to the day of his death, a concept which far transcended a coalition government. He called it 'a government of true national unity and effective action'. Such a government would be drawn not only from the best men and women in Parliament, but also from industry and commerce, trade unions, the universities, the civil service, science, and the armed forces of the Crown — all the most vital elements of the nation.

At a dinner in May 1978 I suggested the formation of an 'Action Society', to propagate Mosley's thesis of the divisiveness of elections as held under the present system, and the futility of party warfare. That Society has helped to attract new subscribers and new contributors to our journal *Action,* and to keep alive the hope that as crisis develops there will emerge enough able men and women prepared to serve our country in a truly national government. It is that hope and that optimism which has prompted me to write this book.

But ten years earlier, in the early months of 1968, I was much occupied in helping Mosley with the final revision of his autobiography. In the book's earlier stages I had paid a number of short visits to France, staying sometimes at the Mosleys' house in Orsay, sometimes at a hotel in the village.

I worked hard on the book all day, and late into the night. In the hotel I ceased typing at a reasonable hour, so as not to disturb the slumbers of other guests, but I would continue with other work on the book for a few more hours, or sometimes throughout the whole night. The one exception to this programme was Sunday, France's traditional day of relaxation, when I would join my dear friends Jerry and Emmy Lehane, the devoted staff of the Mosley household.

They both have the Irish love of horses and horse-racing, and on Sunday afternoons we would go to one or other of the beautiful race-courses near Paris. In England I have never taken any interest in this sport, but in France the beauty of the surroundings and the excitement of the crowd somehow captured my imagination and interest. On one such occasion the staff of the hotel where I was staying entrusted me with money with which to place bets for them on any horses I fancied. At the end of the day I had neither won nor lost, but as a faithful steward I was able to return their talents and account for every franc and centime. To think that I had lived for over fifty years before I learned the French for 'each way'! Truly, one's education is never complete so long as one preserves an open and inquiring mind.

My Life was published by Thomas Nelson on 21 October 1968, and from most of the critics it received the praise it deserved. Among old friends and old opponents who reviewed the book were Professor A.J.P. Taylor, Mr. Norman St John-Stevas, and Mr. Michael Foot. The last named wrote that "the book could cast a dazzling gleam across the whole century ... No rising star in the political firmament ever shone more brightly than Sir Oswald Mosley ... By general consent he could have become the leader of either the Conservative or the Labour Party." I have never for a moment regretted hitching my wagon to that star.

The book enjoyed a great success, and a paperback edition followed. When the firm of Nelson became part of a consortium, both editions were taken over by my own company, Sanctuary Press. *My Life* continues to sell well, fourteen years after its publication, and we still hear of people frustrated by the long waiting-list for it at their public libraries.

The sixties closed for me with my second visit to Germany, to promote the sales of *My Life* there. I flew to Hanover and took a train to Bodenfelde, the nearest station to Lippoldsberg, where I was to stay with Dr. Holle Grimm, daughter of the late Hans Grimm, pre-war poet and author, whose *Answer of a German* — an open letter to the then Archbishop of Canterbury — had been published by Euphorion Books. She lived with her mother in the Klosterhaus, in the heart of particularly beautiful countryside.

My plane and train were late and I arrived at the little wayside station in the early hours of the morning. I took a taxi to Lippoldsberg, where we arrived at an impossible hour for disturbing the Grimms. I had been recommended an hotel, but we found it locked and bolted, and our loud knocking aroused only the guard dog, whose barking was ignored by the hotelier. The obliging taxi driver took me from one hotel to another, until we found one open, and I booked in for what was left of the night.

After breakfast I presented myself at the Klosterhaus, where I was made very welcome by the Grimms, and I spent a most enjoyable week with them, although I had little time to savour their hospitality to the full. I had come to collect long lists of names and addresses of potential customers for our publication, but Dr. Holle had only one list and I had to copy it laboriously by hand. I wrote fast and furiously, all day and every day, and late into each night.

It was glorious summer weather and I was sitting one afternoon by a window which opened on to the courtyard. A child of the village wandered into the yard, where she stood with open mouth and wide brown eyes, staring at the strange figure, head bent, pen moving at speed across and down the page. "Was machen Sie denn ? she inquired. "Schreiben Sie ein Buch?" I assured her that I was not writing a book. She paused to digest this information, and to weigh up other possibilities, before she put to me her next question: "Sind Sie ein Dichter?"

What had made her think I might be a poet? Hans Grimm is still held in high esteem in German literary circles, and once a year, on "Dichtertag", poets and authors come from all over the country, to visit his former study, preserved as a museum, and to pay their respects to his memory. They do not appear to be offended by two of the museum exhibits: letters from Hitler and Goebbels praising Hans Grimm's contribution to German literature.

Chapter Fifteen

From Lippoldsberg I travelled south to Coburg, in Bavaria, to visit Arthur Ehrhardt, who had founded the Nation Europa magazine, which took its title from Mosley's striking 'Europe a Nation' phrase, first used in a speech in 1948.

Ehrhardt had a list of addresses ready to hand to me, so I was spared the ordeal of another bout of copying. But I was subjected to a milder one. He was very deaf and conducted a conversation with the aid of an ancient speaking-trumpet. He would speak into it, insisting on German although he knew some English, and would then pass it across for me to trumpet my reply, while he cupped his ear to the other end. It emitted strange atmospherics, an extraordinary high-pitched whistle, adding to the difficulties of conducting a conversation in a language in which I am far from fluent.

That night I took a train to Frankfurt, where I was to board a plane for London. But I had worked all the previous night and had had a very tiring day, so I fell asleep on the train. When I awoke the compartment was empty except for one man. I asked him how far it was to Frankfurt. "Frankfurt war da", he replied, pointing back in the direction from which we had travelled. I hastily dismounted at the next stop, where I coaxed a taxi driver to take me back to Frankfurt Airport.

It had been a strange experience to visit the new Germany for the first time, with every trace of the alten Tagen obliterated. The best of our old and new friends in that country have no desire to revive them, although they would endorse the sentiment expressed in the opening sentence of this book. But with us they strive now to advance beyond the too narrow nationalism of National Socialism, to the new concept expressed in the title of that Coburg magazine. We strive to advance together towards 'Europe a Nation.'

Chapter Sixteen

The Battle of Cable Street', of Sunday, 4 October 1936, is now firmly established in left-wing mythology and folk-lore, and it looks as if it may never be possible to substitute fact for fiction. In 1969 I was approached by the BBC, who asked my co-operation in making a documentary on this event, as part of their Yesterday's Witness series. I gave them all the help I could, and arranged for them to film an interview with Mosley.

The programme was first shown on BBC 2 in January 1970. It may have been planned to discredit us, but truth will often emerge from the most unexpected quarters. For example, the former communist M.P. Phil Piratin boasted: "We began to make our plans some time before October 4th." Pointing to a street map, he said: "This is where we had prepared to overturn a lorry . . . the instructions were to set it alight." But with masterly communist inefficiency the wrong lorry was overturned and sent up in flames.

A lady who was to have been a leading witness for the prosecution turned out to be invaluable to our defence, as sometimes happens in cases conducted by an inexperienced counsel. East London social worker Miss Edith Ramsay let the proverbial cat out of the bag with her all too frank admission: "I remember the communist posters advising us all to turn out and stop the march . . . Communists from all over England possibly. Certainly large numbers came from Glasgow, and there were Glaswegians at Gardiner's Corner."

Yet the myth has survived that there had been, in a delightful phrase that used to crop up in almost every issue of the pre-war *Daily Worker*, 'a spontaneous uprising of the angry British workers against Fascism.'

It cannot be sufficiently emphasised that the 'battle' that day was between a communist mob, largely imported from outside London, and the police, who were unable to disperse them and clear the streets for our march. The then Commissioner of Police, Sir Philip Game, was in personal charge of the police operations, and eventually informed Mosley that the march could not take place. Mosley, as always, obeyed police instructions and gave orders for the marchers to turn about and march away in good order. Only isolated Blackshirts (such as Tommy Moran, as described in Chapter 13) waylaid by the mob on their way to the rendezvous, were involved in the 'Battle'. The final absurdity of the left-wing myth is that the 'Battle' ended in such a glorious victory over Mosley that 'he never dared show his face in East London again.' What are the facts?

By the following Wednesday, the coaches which Miss Ramsay admitted seeing had long returned to Leeds and Glasgow, and Mosley led a triumphant march through East London, to four large and enthusiastic meetings. Five months later, in the LCC election of March 1937, Mosley's candidates polled an average of nearly 20 per cent of the total votes recorded (23 per cent in Bethnal Green). This on a register that penalised us, as at that time only householders were eligible to vote in local elections.

Young people, who formed the bulk of our support, were largely disenfranchised, the acute housing shortage forcing them to live with their parents or in-laws, even after they had married. Again and again, in letters to national, provincial and local newspapers, I have corrected this silly lie of a 'Battle' against Mosley in Cable Street, and a 'victory' over him. Yet the Left's propaganda machine keeps the myth alive

The council of the London Borough of Tower Hamlets has recently contributed, from the pockets of the long-suffering ratepayers, to the sum of £20,000 awarded to an artist to paint a graphic mural of a 'battle' which never took place. The BBC programme faded out with a shot of me speaking at a post-war street-comer meeting in Bethnal Green, with the commentator observing sagely that "it still goes on." Indeed it does.

April 1975 was an important month for us. On 3 April Robert Skidelsky's biography *Oswald Mosley* was published by Macmillans, and on the same date my own company Sanctuary Press re-issued Mosley's *My Life* in hardback and paperback. Skidelsky's book excited as much attention as had Mosley's on its first appearance, and its publishers rushed out a second edition within a month of Mosley's death in December 1980. It is a long book — over five hundred pages — so anyone who reads that and *My Life*, and my own modest effort, will know what the policies were that Mosley so consistently and determinedly advocated.

Skidelsky is a not unfriendly critic of Mosley, but he writes with the objectivity of the professional historian. Yet when the book appeared left-wing critics accused him of 'white-washing' Mosley, an allegation which Skidelsky explains away in the introduction to the second edition of his book. The first edition, he explains, "was written against a background of unhistorical, anti-Mosley myth-making", so his endeavours to expose these fables may have given the impression of special pleading. He adds that if he were writing a Mosley biography today he would make certain modifications. This book will always remain an essential commentary on Mosley, and an invaluable source for future researchers to tap.

The publication of the Skidelsky book and the re-issue of *My Life* broke temporarily the television boycott of Mosley, which had been in force since the war, except for a few programmes in the years immediately following 1968. In a short period he made five television appearances, in three countries. A short interview on the BBC's 'Today' programme aroused so much interest that a fuller half-hour version of it was transmitted at a later date. An interview with Ludovic Kennedy on the BBC 'Midweek' programme ran for twenty-three minutes. On 12 April 1975

Chapter Sixteen

Mosley appeared in Dublin on the Irish television 'Late-late Night Show', and on 14 April an extremely fair interview with him by Eileen O'Brien was published in the *Irish Times*. Finally, Mosley appeared on Scottish Television on April 18, and took part in a Sunday lunch-hour radio programme.

Mosley and I appeared on television on consecutive nights in February 1976. Part of my programme was recorded in a Bethnal Green pub, after shots of my old friend Sid Bailey selling *Action* in the Sunday morning market. The pub was packed, noisy with shouted orders and animated conversation. A microphone was clipped to my tie, the continuity girl called "Scene 1, take 1", and I had to think quickly how I could make myself heard above the hubbub. I took a deep breath and announced in a loud voice: "It seems to me that Sir Oswald Mosley has been proved right in everything he has said!"

Can there really be such a silence that you can hear the proverbial pin dropping to the floor? Yes, and there was on this occasion, as a deathly hush fell over the lunch-time festivities.

One voice broke the silence with a shout of "Rubbish!", but then strangers converged on us from all sides, assuring us that they had been pre-war Blackshirts, and that Mosley had been right, and that I was right to say so. I wonder what would have happened if I had substituted the name of Harold Wilson or Edward Heath for that of Oswald Mosley. Would I have had to run for my life, instead of enjoying the typical hospitality of an East London pub until closing-time?

On 16 November 1976 Sir Oswald Mosley celebrated his eightieth birthday. It fell on a Tuesday, and the next few days were truly memorable. On the Wednesday evening he appeared on the BBC 'Tonight' programme, and gave his usual dynamic performance, belying his age. On the Friday I travelled with him to Manchester for a dinner organised in his honour in an hotel which had formerly been the old Mosley family home, Hough

End, built in 1596 by Sir Nicholas Mosley, then Lord Mayor of London. There are several restaurants in this hotel, and the manager kindly put at our disposal the appropriately named Mosley Suite.

We concluded the birthday celebrations with a London dinner on the Saturday evening. I had placed Lady Mosley on his right, and beside her two 'old girls' of her Holloway Prison days, class of 1940. One was my old friend Fay Taylour, former star of speedway and motor racing. (In the early, pre-war days of speedway women had been allowed to compete, and Fay had beaten all the leading male riders, breaking a number of track records). When I last saw her she was still a very attractive woman. She told me that a journalist once asked why such a beautiful girl had never married, but had taken up such a rough sport as speedway. She replied: "I was engaged once, but he broke off the engagement and asked me if I wanted to buy his motorbike!" During 'The Battle of Ridley Road' Fay used to drive me home after the meetings in a rather magnificent Jaguar car.

I never experienced the slightest fear at these meetings, however many bricks were flying, but I used to be terrified by Fay's driving, and would clutch the seat with both hands, as she took every corner on two wheels. Years later (when she had returned from selling sports cars to film stars in Hollywood) I was talking to her about this magnificent car, and I was surprised to learn that it had not been hers. She told me that in Holloway she had met among the prisoners a rather high-class call-girl, and when they were released she had given her friend driving lessons in return for the occasional use of her Jaguar.

The Special Branch must have been quietly amused when they first noted its number and checked on its owner. 'Fabulous Fay' indeed, as she was always known in speedway and motor-racing circles. By the mid-seventies the ban imposed by corrupt councils was almost complete, but I won a minor victory against one of them, in my battle for free speech. I had complained to

Chapter Sixteen

the Commissioner for Local Administration, popularly known as 'the local Ombudsman', about the refusal of the London Borough of Ealing, in which I am a householder and ratepayer, to hire me Ealing Town Hall for a third public meeting, after two had been conducted in perfect order. The Ombudsman found the council guilty of 'maladministration', and ruled that I "had been caused injustice"

His long report set out the facts at considerable length. In brief summary, my application for a meeting in July 1974 had been rejected. I had asked that my letter seeking an explanation should be put before the Amenities Committee, but the Town Clerk replied that he had "consulted the Chairman of the Committee, who concurs with my view that as this was a Committee decision no further action can be taken." The Town Clerk later admitted that council regulations clearly state that "action taken by the chairman should be reported to the next meeting of the committee."

In January 1975 I applied for use of the hall for a referendum meeting on British membership of the EEC, and on April 7 the appropriate committee recommended that my application be granted, but I was not informed. The council considered this recommendation on April 29, when they adjourned it for "further consideration" on June 23, thus making it impossible for a meeting to be held before the national referendum on June 5. The committee again recommended that my application be granted, but the council rejected this on July 15.

The Ombudsman's report concluded: "The considerable delay by the Council. . . and their failure to keep the complainant informed . . . was maladministration which caused injustice to him ..." In March 1977 the Ombudsman issued a second report, stating that he was "not satisfied with the action the authority have taken or propose to take" on his first report. "In short, the Council have, to my mind, repeated the maladministration which caused the original injustice."

He continued to press the council and I eventually received an apology from it, but no lifting of its ban on free speech. Throughout the controversy the Conservatives, then in opposition on the council, had spoken in favour of free speech. In May 1979 they gained control of the Council, and immediately rejected an application from me for the use of the Town Hall! I wrote personally to the new Conservative Leader of the Council, Mrs. Beatrice Howard, but she refused to lift the ban. Yet in 1975 she had written to me: "I regret the Council has made this decision and, as you are probably aware, it was on a majority vote of the Labour Party. My colleagues and I supported a motion that your organisation should be allowed the use of the hall, not because we agree with your views but because we believe in the freedom to express views publicly providing there is no incitement to violence. There is little I can do at the moment but I will continue to support your right to hire the public halls." This noble attitude no doubt won votes for Conservative candidates in the elections of May 1979, but having won it, by false pretences, the good lady and her colleagues showed their true colours. Put not your trust in Conservative councillors, or M.P's.

In addition, I was now effectively barred from the universities, with a few honourable exceptions which defied the infamous ban placed upon me by the sordid little left-wing clique which had gained control of the Executive of the National Union of Students. This was a tremendous compliment to my record of successes in university debates over the years (I had by this time won two of my last three), but the decision had to be challenged.

I wrote to the 1974 President John Randall, challenging him to a public debate, but he did not offer even the courtesy of a reply. On June 4 of that year he took part in a BBC4 radio 'phone-in' programme. I telephoned a question, repeating my challenge, early in the evening, and my call was noted. I then sat with one ear to the radio, and the other near my telephone, but no call came through.

Chapter Sixteen

The harshness of these struggles is from time to time softened by agreeable evenings in the company of old and new friends. I have, for example, particular affection for old stalwarts in East Anglia, such as Mrs. Dimond, Mrs. Flowerdew, and Mr. and Mrs. Hoggarth. We spent a particularly happy evening one year in celebration of the birthday of our mutual friend Ronald Creasy. He was one of the heroes of the Tithe War of the thirties, when Blackshirts had helped local farmers who were resisting the seizure of their farm-stock by the bailiffs. The party was held in the beautiful Scole Inn, on the Suffolk-Norfolk border, and after it we all returned to the Creasy home, the even more beautiful Cranley Manor, at Eye. Such friendships and events make our years of struggle so rewarding, whatever the final outcome may be.

On the same happy note, on August 27, 1977, I attended the wedding of a member of the Directory of Union Movement, Dan Harmston and Lucia Vallentin, a charming Canadian girl of Dutch origin, at the Church of the Immaculate Conception, in Mayfair's Farm Street. Dan Harmston had been a popular figure in the boxing world, until trouble from cut eyes had forced him to retire from the sport. He had led his fellow Smithfield Market porters in an anti-immigration march, not in support of the views of Enoch Powell, as the Press wrongly reported, but of those of his hero Oswald Mosley. His friends all knew where his allegiance lay, and they had dubbed him "Big Dan, the Mosley Man !"

On the day of the wedding I alighted from a taxi at the church door as Dan and some of his friends from the world of boxing and Smithfield Market were posing for photographs, before entering the church to await the bride's arrival. My cabbie was intrigued at the sight of these burly men in immaculate morning dress, grey toppers in their large hands. He was convinced that this was the society wedding of the year, and he drove away shaking his head in disbelief at my explanation. We went on from the church to a highly enjoyable reception at Jack Straw's Castle, on Hampstead Heath. Happy also, has been the experience of meeting many colourful characters, too numerous to name. One example springs to mind: the guest speaker at our Action dinner in December 1975 was Joey Martin-Martin, much in the news in that period as a member of the Middle Class Association, which later became the Voice of the Independent Centre.

At the dinner he entertained us with a lively and witty speech, on which I managed to concentrate in spite of sitting next to his glamorous wife, the beautiful model Vanya, the Sun newspaper Page 3 girl of that year. She was, I may add, fully and decorously clothed on that occasion. Even serious politics need not be dull.

Chapter Seventeen

"Whenever I see a newspaper contents bill with the words 'Peer's daughter. . . ' I know that one of you gels has been up to something." In Ned Sherrin's musical The Mitford Girls the remark is attributed to Lord Redesdale, but I have always heard them ascribed to Lady Redesdale. They referred, of course, to the famous daughters of the Redesdales, six in all: Deborah, Diana, Jessica, Nancy, Pamela, Unity — to list them in alphabetical order.

I went to see the musical in the last week of its 14-week run at the Globe Theatre, where it had been transferred from the Chichester Festival. Patricia Hodge, who played both Lady Redesdale and Nancy Mitford in the musical, commented on the unfair treatment it had received from the critics, who concentrated on the 'unsuitability' of the theme, and made no comment on the enthusiasm of the first-night audience, unique in the long experience of the theatre's manager.

Denigration of this remarkable family is nothing new. It was given a good airing by David Pryce-Jones in his absurd book Unity Mitford: A Quest, published in November 1976. How thorough and searching was his 'quest'? In a letter to the Times of 18 November 1976 three of the sisters — Pamela, Diana, and Deborah — claimed that they held letters from "a number of people quoted in the book saying that they have been misquoted." Extracts from some of these letters were published in the Sunday Times of 21 November 1976, and in these most who had originally helped Pryce-Jones with his research later expressed regret at having done so. Pryce-Jones naturally rejected all their allegations and complaints.

The campaign of distortion was renewed in March 1981, when the BBC presented a television play based on the Pryce-Jones book.

That evening the London New Standard published an interview with Pryce-Jones, by journalist Sue Summers, from which his sense of objectivity may be tested. For example, describing a television confrontation between him and Sir Oswald Mosley he said of Mosley: "At one point he was in such a rage his eyes went completely animal red." In reply to this absurdity (and to the equally silly story in the book about Unity tying a grass-snake to a lavatory chain to frighten her nanny) I wrote in a letter to the Standard: "Unless there were a colour-fault on my television set at no time did Mosley's eyes turn 'completely animal red'... He remained his urbane self when challenging Pryce-Jones on the silly lie about the grass-snake . . . When Pryce-Jones insisted that he had met the nanny concerned Mosley could not challenge the statement. Only later did he learn that it would have been quite impossible for the two to have met."

But 'distortion' of the Mitfords has not always been the fault of their detractors. One of the sisters has been innocently responsible for creating a false picture — Nancy Mitford in her novel The Pursuit of Love, where Lord Redesdale is thinly disguised as Uncle Matthew, or 'Farve.' Pryce-Jones chose to take the book seriously, and to perpetuate the legend that a cruel Farve used to set a pack of fierce hounds on the terrified girls. In reality, the girls loved to play a sort of hide-and-seek with one tame old bloodhound.

Nancy's teasing article about U and non-U English was taken equally seriously by those who wished to portray the sisters as snobs who had deliberately cultivated an affected accent and manner. They were, of course, born and bred with 'the Mitford voice', and it is as unfair to criticise them for this as it would be to sneer at a Cockney or Lancashire accent. What people say is much more important than how they say it. What are they really like? I never met Jessica, Nancy, or Unity, and I naturally know Diana better than the other two. But I have found all three charming, and so natural and unaffected that no-one who had ever met them would again take *The Pursuit of Love* seriously. Deborah, Duchess of Devonshire, the dignified figure of television interviews at Chatsworth, unbends in conversation. One of her 'teases' is that she has never read a book. Quite untrue, of course. I once urged her to write one, and stressed that she need not read it, but only write it. She has now written a book, which was for weeks in the best seller lists.

Pamela was a former wife of Professor Derek Jackson, the distinguished atomic scientist who died in France early last year. I last met her in the London Hospital, when she arrived to visit Diana, a patient there after a brain tumour. I do not know either of these sisters well, but my affection for Diana embraces everyone who is close to her.

Diana's autobiography, *A Life of Contrasts*, was published by Hamish Hamilton on 14 April 1977. In my review in *Action* I said that literary critics insist that it is a grave fault for a biographer to be prejudiced for or against his subject, and I commented that this rule should apply also to reviewers, whose personal prejudices so often distort their work. But the rule would have barred me from reviewing the book "because I must plead guilty to a strong prejudice in favour of Lady Mosley."

My review was a highly favourable one, but I trust I did not exaggerate the merits of what seemed to me a remarkable book. The 'contrasts' of the title are many and varied; the first to appear are on the dust-jacket: on the front a photograph of the author's beautiful house at Orsay, on the back the grim fortress of the old Holloway Prison. (A wit observed that he did not much care for the little house on the front, but loved the splendid mansion on the back).

On May 12, Lady Mosley was the guest of honour at a Foyle's literary luncheon at the Dorchester Hotel. Miss Christina Foyle had chosen a most distinguished Chairman in Brigadier the Rt. Hon. Sir John Smythe, Bart, V.C., M.C., who praised Lady Mosley's book highly, and said of Sir Oswald: "He is a great orator and leader of men, whose footprints are indelible on the sands of time." Lord Boothby said he would never forget Mosley's resignation speech from the Labour Government of 1929—1931, and described him as having possessed "the makings of the greatest politician the country ever had." If Sir Oswald and he had been in charge of the country there would have been no Second World War. Sir Arthur Bryant, the historian, spoke well of the book and its ingredients of "the two things which really matter in life — love and courage."

In her reply Lady Mosley claimed her hearers' indulgence as she had never spoken in public before. "We already have one orator in the family." But her maiden speech was replete with wit and humour, as in her description of Holloway Prison as "the only interesting bit of architecture in that part of London." But she would not be contributing to any fund for the preservation of its Victorian gate-house.

In Manchester days I often noticed on the fringe of the crowd at my meetings a certain Police Sergeant Robert Mark. Many promotions and some twenty-eight years later we met again, at the Army and Navy Stores, where he autographed for me a copy of his autobiography In the Office of Constable, which had just been published. I had browsed through a copy and had found a reference to me and to those Manchester meetings; and to those 'extremists of the Left, whose counter arguments were often expressed by throwing bricks or other persuasive impedimenta'. I placed my copy of his book on the desk in front of him, and said: "You won't remember me, Sir Robert, although you have a passing reference to me in your book." He looked up and exclaimed: "Jeffrey Hamm!" It was a remarkable feat of memory for such a busy man, and it was agreeable to talk to him for a few minutes after so many years.

In a previous chapter I have remarked that I have never paid any more attention to the few bouquets I have received over the years than I have to the many more brickbats hurled in my direction;

but in the conversation that day and in a subsequent exchange of letters Sir Robert paid me an extraordinary compliment in saying that he had always thought of me as "a very brave man." This was high praise coming from a very brave man indeed.

This may be a convenient point at which to comment on my attitude towards the police which I have discussed with them upon occasion. As I see it, we have two distinct jobs: theirs is to 'keep the Queen's peace', and mine to propagate ideas, by any lawful means. As we stand for a well-manned, well paid, and well equipped police force to maintain law and order there should be no conflict of interests between us.

On the rare occasions when there has been a difference of opinion I have much regretted it; but I have almost invariably placed the blame on bad law rather than on any individual police officer. Many of them share our dislike of the Public Order Act, which in fact contributed to much public disorder by taking away our political uniform and depriving us of our former right to steward outdoor meetings. Until the Act was passed, what Mosley's opponents called his 'private army' maintained at outdoor meetings the same order that his stewards preserved indoors.

Today we concede that 'private armies' are undesirable; but in forbidding them the law should at the same time guarantee freedom of speech for all. There is now a strong case for banning all street demonstrations, because they place an intolerable burden on over-stretched police resources and on the rate-payers, while considerable inconvenience is caused to the general public. But every public hall in the country should be made available, by law, to every applicant for its hire.

I have always been scrupulously careful never to name any police officer with whom I have been friendly, as the Left would seize on this, and brand him as yet another 'Fascist pig.' For this reason a certain former Special Branch officer shall still remain anonymous. One Saturday afternoon some years ago I arrived at the Old Deer Park to find that a London Welsh rugby match had been cancelled because of frost. I thought there might be a match at Twickenham, as the high stands there sometimes protect the pitch. As I crossed the road to catch a bus to Twickenham I met this Special Branch officer and told him where I was going. He said he would come with me, and we got on the bus together. We carried on an animated conversation on politics until the conductor's "All change!" made us aware that we had long passed Twickenham, and were alone on the bus, which had reached its terminus at Teddington.

My companion said teasingly that if we had gone another mile I would have converted him, and he would have joined us. He told me later that there had been much leg-pulling at Scotland Yard the following Monday morning, when he described our journey to his colleagues.

Some time ago I met him again on an agreeable rugby weekend at Weston-super-Mare, and I told him I proposed mentioning him in a book I was writing. He went round his wide circle of friends in the bar exclaiming: "I'm famous! I'm going to be mentioned in Jeffrey's book!" I hope he will enjoy reading this.

Rugby is one of the passions of my life. I had to give up playing at an early age, because I was teaching in schools where it was frowned upon; and for years I worked on Saturdays and had no time even to watch matches. But eventually I became more of a free agent, and I joined London Welsh Rugby Club. By great good fortune I joined at the beginning of a golden era in its history.

The inimitable John Dawes had been appointed club captain, a position he held for six seasons, going on to captain Wales and the 1971 Lions, before becoming coach to the Welsh team and later National Coaching Organiser for Wales. In the same period the club was joined by some of the most famous players of the seventies, and made rugby history when six of its members were included in the 1971 British Lions party of thirty to tour New Zealand: "J.P.R.", Gerald Davies, Mervyn Davies, John Taylor, and Mike Roberts, led by John Dawes as captain. When Geoff Evans went out to New Zealand as a replacement, and the club representation was raised to seven, our cup was indeed flowing over. John Dawes was the first Welshman to captain a British Lions team, and the 1971 Lions were the first to win a test series in New Zealand. My traditional Welsh modesty forbids my belabouring the point. A few years ago I started to learn Welsh, at the weekly classes at the London Welsh Association in Grays Inn Road. At first I found it a very difficult language, the most difficult I had ever attempted to master; but I have persevered, and I can now understand much of what is said to me in Welsh, and can say a little in return. At least when asked if I speak the language, I can reply: Tipyn bach. Rydw i'n dysgu Cymraeg — A little. I'm learning Welsh.

I seek relaxation also in long Sunday afternoon walks, the occasional visit to the theatre, reading, and listening to records; but politics remain my first love. The first dinner held by our newly-formed Action Society was held in December 1978, and Colin Cross was our distinguished guest speaker. I had come to know him well when he visited our offices to research for his book The Fascists in Britain, published in 1961. Referring to the book in his speech, he said he felt rather as Daniel must have felt on entering the lions' den, and he courageously admitted: "The last chapter was not strong on research; it was merely the journalist in me wanting to summarise very briefly what had happened to this movement of the thirties." He ended his speech by forecasting that when the history of British Union comes to be written "the idealism which in many cases animated it is not going to be forgotten."

In 1977 I had been saddened by the death of my old friend Henry Williamson, who had suffered much for his loyalty to Mosley. After the war, when he was creating, as many thought, his masterpiece, the fifteen-volume novel known collectively as

Chapter Seventeen

A Chronicle of Ancient Sunlight, his books frequently received dismissive reviews, or none at all. The degrees committee of the university of which he was a signal benefactor twice vetoed the proposal to award him an honorary doctorate. In spite of representations made, unknown to him, by friends and admirers, his name was not put forward for recognition in New Year or Birthday honours' lists. I am proud to have known Henry, to have numbered him among my friends, and to be a member of the Henry Williamson Society, formed to perpetuate his memory.

Oswald Mosley and Henry Williamson were almost exactly the same age, and both belonged to that 'Phoenix Generation' (the title of one of Henry's novels) which had been through the first World War in the front line. Williamson had always kept himself in good physical trim, and he remained active and energetic almost until he was eighty. With Mosley it was the same, but at a buffet supper given by Action Society in 1980, to celebrate the publication of Lady Mosley's biography of the Duchess of Windsor, he seemed to have aged considerably. He was supposed not to stand for longer than was necessary, and for most of the evening he remained seated, clearly enjoying himself talking to old friends.

Later in the evening he rose, to make a five-minute speech, in a clear, strong voice, quite in his customary forceful style. In this speech he made a strong plea that all should now sink their political differences to contribute to the common task of seeking ways and means of preventing the planet from being blown up by accident. With the ever-proliferating stock-piles of nuclear weapons this had become the urgent issue of our time. He did not think that anyone would unleash a nuclear holocaust intentionally, but it could happen through some accident. For this reason, he said, the West must talk to the Russians — and keep talking. As recently as March 1982 this advice was ignored, when the Brezhnev proposals were arbitrarily dismissed by British and American leaders.

I have written only of British politics, with some references to Europe, but Action Society has already attracted the support of peoples outside our continent. Good friends like Hamilton Barrett of California, and Howard Matthews of Florida are working, as I write, on a project for me to lecture in the United States, on our concept of a Europe independent of both communist Russia and capitalist America, but not hostile to either. Our respective systems must learn to co-exist, if mankind is not to perish.

It was fitting that the last message of the man who had striven to prevent the war of 1939—1945 should have been a message of peace. In the early hours of Wednesday, 3rd December, 1980, I received a telephone call from France telling me that Sir Oswald Mosley had died in his sleep during the night. At the time I was too shocked to appreciate the full significance of the tragic news, but my spirits were revived even on the solemn occasion of his cremation in the Pere Lachaise cemetery in Paris, a few days later, as his sons from both his marriages read some of his favourite poetry, including those inspiring lines of Arthur Clough which begin: "Say not the struggle naught availeth ..."

Mosley was a phenomenon. He achieved his own definition of greatness, 'the complete man', in politics and unique economic thinking, in sport in his youth, with fencing and boxing, war service in the Flanders trenches and in the Royal Flying Corps, a deep interest in philosophy. Always a man of culture, he was the true aristocrat: a man of the people.

I may claim to have known the real Mosley, as distinct from the public image, better than anyone outside his family circle. What was he really like? Did he have no faults at all? My considered reply would be: none which could be weighed seriously against his virtues and superb qualities.

He was a hard task-master, and I was not always too pleased with him when I had eventually got to bed late at night after a strenuous day, and the telephone would ring at one or two o'clock in the morning. But my irritation would be short-lived, speedily disarmed by his polite inquiry: "I hope I'm not ringing you too late?"

He was perhaps a poor judge of character, assuming that everyone was as honest as he, or overlooking their faults if they possessed qualities he admired. This sometimes led him into trusting the likeable rogue, and landed us in difficulties from which I was expected to extricate him, having previously warned him of the possible consequences and having my warnings airily swept aside.

His opponents accused him of arrogance and I could tell tales out of school which would appear to substantiate this, but the allegation is not true. I recall meeting him at Manchester's Piccadilly Station. We walked out into the forecourt, and without hesitation he stepped into a taxi. A railway policeman remonstrated: "You can't do that, sir. There's a long queue for taxis." "Queue, queue? replied Mosley. "There's too much of that damned nonsense in this country !" And he was away before the astonished policeman could collect his thoughts and think of a suitable reply.

When I was taking the page-proofs of The European to Paris each month the Mosleys were on one occasion on holiday in Normandy, and Lady Mosley asked me to meet them at an hotel in Le Havre "about lunchtime." I went over on the night boat, arrived in Le Havre at breakfast time, and went to the hotel about midday. I bought a drink, and awaited their arrival.

An hour passed, with no sign of the Mosleys. The patron asked me if I were ordering lunch, but I declined, anticipating lunching with them when they arrived. I bought a second drink, and sipped it very slowly. All the other guests had lunched, and the patron and his wife ate theirs in the bar, aggravating the pangs of hunger which were beginning to gnaw. At three o'clock they arrived, with apologies for the delay, but with no word of lunch.

"We have a lot of work to do", said Sir Oswald, as he ushered me into the lounge. "I think we'll have that table over here", and we moved it to a convenient spot.

He began to dictate letters, and I typed them furiously. If other guests dared to disturb us with their chatter they were frozen into silence, until they tip-toed out of the lounge. The patron came in to ask if we were taking a room, but he was waved aside. His wife entered, but she met the same fate. Late in the afternoon Lady Mosley noticed that I looked a little wan, and she ordered some coffee and rolls for me, but his look of disapproval at such an interruption to our work deterred me from taking more than a sip and a bite.

By middle evening our work was completed, and he ordered a bottle of wine. He could not stay to drink it with me, and he prepared to leave. His final comment was: "I don't think we'll come here again. It was rather noisy!" He picked up his favourite trilby, which he always called his 'Frenchman's hat', waved the patron and his wife a cheerful " 'Revoir, m'sieur, madame", and left them sharing the astonishment of that Manchester railway policeman.

Was this arrogance or contempt? No, it was just the supreme self-confidence of a man conscious of his great talents, driving himself hard and demanding equal dedication and devotion to duty from all who served him, impatient at any petty impediments to the grand purpose. None who shared his faith in 'the vision splendid' ever took offence at this attitude to life. I was proud to serve him, in a cause to which I shall dedicate the rest of my own life.

On a lighter note, Mosley's handwriting was notoriously difficult to read. Apocryphal is the story that someone took one of his letters into a chemist's shop and emerged with a bottle of medicine. True is the report that of the large pre-war staff at British Union headquarters only his secretary George

Sutton could decipher his memoranda. Each morning a queue would form outside Sutton's office, recipients of these strange inscriptions come to have them interpreted. There was some slight embarrassment one morning, when Sutton started to decode a memorandum, only to discover that it opened with the admonition: 'Don't show Sutton this."

Towards the end of Mosley's life it was said that only three people could decipher this extraordinary handwriting: Lady Mosley, Mosley's solicitor Jack Lane, and myself. I once received a telephone call from Lord Boothby to say he had received a note from 'Tom' Mosley, but could read only a few words of it. He had, he said, deciphered "tell them", but "I don't know who the 'them' might be, or what I have to tell them." I volunteered to go to his flat to assist him, and at one glance I saw that he was not obliged to "tell them" anything. Mosley was going on a journey, returning on such and such a date. "Till then" he could be contacted through me.

I have mentioned few friends by name in this book since the inclusion of some might embarrass them; and, in any case, to select a few from the many would be invidious. I have loved them all, including many who have disagreed with me, but on questions of strategy and tactics rather than on basic principles. Perhaps I am rather more fond of them than of those who have always agreed with me, because they have been the fleas on the back of this old dog, irritating and stimulating him to examine all his pre-conceived ideas, and to put them to the test of cross-examination.

Perhaps 'devil's advocate' would be a more appropriate expression than 'flea' for one of the ablest of these, Peter Wallis, who has reviewed books for Action, and contributed from time to time his excellent In the Margin column. I have known him since he went from school into the Army for his National Service before he went up to Cambridge. I much enjoy his company, because he never seems to agree with me on any subject. He tries to debunk all my theories, and to deflate my ego, in case I am ever in danger of suffering from hubris. I thank him, and all the many whose friendship has sustained me through the years of struggle.

Sometimes at our dinners we drink a toast to 'Absent Friends', and we include among them the many who have died over the years. It was fortunate that British Union was largely a movement of youth, so that many of its members survived the second World War, and are alive today. Sadly, though, many others have died, and I have had to write too many, far too many, obituary notices for Action. It would be as invidious to recall the names of some of the dead as it would of the living, but perhaps I may be allowed to mention just four, who were members of our post-war staff, and with whom I worked closely.

The first to die was E.D. 'Ernie' Hart, a master of research, with a phenomenal memory for facts and figures. The second was Raven Thomas, of whom I have already written some small tribute. The third was Hector McKechnie, organiser of so many great pre-war meetings, including that at Earls Court. I attended his funeral at Frinton, with our mutual old friends 'Inky' and Louise Irvine. We made the occasion one of jollity rather than solemnity, because we knew that was the spirit of the real 'Mac' we knew and loved, beneath his somewhat haughty exterior. So we were pleased when by happy coincidence the cortege passed his favourite pub, where he so much enjoyed his whisky: neat.

It was the haughty Mac who once waved aside a waiter who was trying to pour water into his glass of whisky. "Water?" asked Mac. "That's for washing in." So when the priest at the graveside sprinkled Mac's coffin with holy water one of us irreverently muttered that Mac had never seen so much of that element in his lifetime.

Mac had at one time been British Consul in a South American republic, and he loved to regale us with stories of his exploits there. My favourite was that of his sleeping off a hang-over one morning, after drinking not wisely but too well the night before. He was awakened by a great commotion under his bedroom window, so he staggered out of bed in his pyjamas, on to the balcony. As soon as he appeared the local town band struck up the British National Anthem. Mac had forgotten it was the King's birthday, but the locals had remembered, and had come to present their compliments to the British consul. "I felt such a fool", said the haughty Mac, "standing there in my pyjamas, taking the Royal Salute!"

The fourth to die was Ann Good, Mosley's private secretary for years, devoted to him, and to Lady Mosley, whose internment in Holloway Prison she had shared. Her loveable qualities made us forgive her everything, including the bag of strong-smelling fish she used to bring to the office, to take home to her beloved cats. It was a sad, and yet somehow a happy duty, to attend her funeral in Ipswich, with Ronald Creasy and Emily Dimond.

In the course of recording the BBC Tonight programme in February 1976 John Pitman put to me a question which, together with my answer, had to be cut out in the editing. He asked me: "Don't people often say to you, 'You're wasting your time, Jeffrey'? I replied: "Yes, candid friends often say that to me. But what are they really asking me to do? To give up what I believe to be right, because it is difficult, and to take up something I know to be wrong, because it is easier. That seems to be so absurd that I must reject it out of hand." I added that if I were on my deathbed I would not say that I had wasted my life, but would be more likely to say that I had had a hard life, but an interesting and exciting one. I had tried, I had 'had a go'.

After he had switched off his recording machine Mr. Pitman asked me: "Would you really say that on your deathbed?" I laughed, and replied that it would depend on how much breath I had left at the end of my life. Dr. Johnson has assured us that the contemplation of death by a man 'concentrates his mind wonderfully.' However, it might be wiser for me to sum up my simple, basic philosophy now, while I am in full possession of all my faculties, and in that context my remark to Mr. Pitman was true. I would have to admit that my private life and practice no doubt fall very far short of the precepts of my religious faith.

In the same way, I may at times have failed to live up to the standards set by my political beliefs, occasionally putting private pleasure before public duty. But in my private as in my political life I have continued to believe in principles; and sometimes principles, whether divine or human, seem almost to transcend the possibility of practice. At least I have tried. I would like to think that I might deserve to have on my tombstone, as my final epitaph, the words of St. Paul:

> 'I have fought the fight to the end,
> I have run the race to the finish,
> I have kept the faith.'

END